Running the Curve Life's 400-Meter Race

A Journey Through Life's Stages, One Sprint at a Time

By Jiles Smith II

PUBLISHED BY: ISHAM MEDIA GROUP, LLC

TABLE OF CONTENTS

Dedication

This book is dedicated to three extraordinary men who not only shaped my path as an athlete but also taught me invaluable lessons about life, leadership, and the relentless pursuit of excellence. Their influence extends far beyond the track, and their wisdom continues to guide me in every endeavor.

To Rod Barksdale, my friend, teammate, and brother in spirit. From the dusty tracks of Compton High School to the competitive arenas at the University of Arizona, you were more than a teammate; you were a partner in the grind, a source of unwavering support, and a living example of what it means to push beyond limits. Our shared struggles and triumphs taught me the power of camaraderie and the importance of having someone who believes in you, even when the finish line seems out of reach. Thank you for being a constant reminder that success is sweeter when shared.

To Coach Curtis Seymore, a pillar of strength and dedication. For 40 years, you poured your heart into Compton High School, shaping not just athletes but lives. You saw potential in a 16-year-old Jiles that I didn't always see in myself, and you never hesitated to push me to be better, even when I resisted. Your selflessness, patience, and unwavering belief in your athletes taught me that true leadership is about sacrifice and service. You showed me that the road to success is paved with hard work, discipline, and an unshakable commitment to excellence. Thank you for putting up with me, for believing in me, and for showing me what it means to lead with heart.

To Coach Willie Williams, a mentor, a guide, and a visionary. At the University of Arizona, you didn't just coach athletes, you built champions, both on and off the track. Your ability to see the bigger picture, to instill discipline, and to inspire greatness transformed not only my athletic career but also my approach to life. You taught me that success is not a destination but a journey, and that the true measure of a person lies in their determination, resilience, and commitment to their goals. Thank you for showing me that the road to success is never easy, but it is always worth it.

To Rod, Coach Seymore, and Coach Williams - three of the greatest men and leaders I have ever known, thank you for showing me that the road to success is not about shortcuts or luck, but about hard work, determination, and an unyielding commitment to becoming the best version of myself. Your lessons have stayed with me long after the races were run, and your legacy continues to inspire me every day. This book is a testament to the values you instilled in me, and I hope it honors the impact you've had on my life.

With deepest gratitude,
Jiles Smith II

Foreword

by Rod Barksdale

I've known Jiles Smith for a long time, long enough to say without hesitation that he has always been one of the most disciplined, intentional, and purpose-driven people I've ever met. Long before titles, certifications, and leadership roles, Jiles stood out because of the way he approached life. He worked hard, he studied the details, and he carried himself with a quiet focus that made everybody around him better. You couldn't miss it.

Those qualities came alive on the track. Track and field has a way of revealing who you are when nobody's watching. The practices, the pain, the pressure of competition—there's no hiding your character. Jiles learned early that success isn't shaped on the straightaways. It's shaped in the curve, where your form, your discipline, and your belief get tested all at once. That lesson stayed with him long after he stopped competing. It shows up in his coaching, in his leadership, and in the way he mentors young people and adults today.

I've seen Jiles give his time to athletes who needed direction. I've seen him teach coaches how to lead with clarity and heart. I've seen him walk into boardrooms, schools, and city departments with the same steady mindset he had on the track: focus on the fundamentals, stay true to your values, and finish strong. Everything he teaches comes from lived experience—not theory, not guesswork, but real life.

This book, *Running the Curve*, is Jiles in written form. It's honest. It's practical. It's rooted in humility and strength. And it reminds you that the curve isn't the part you fear—it's the part that prepares you. Jiles shows you how to handle the tough turns in life with the same discipline he learned as a young runner in Compton and refined over decades of coaching, consulting, and personal growth.

If you know Jiles, you'll hear his voice on every page. If you don't know him yet, you'll feel like you do by the time you finish.

The lessons in this book aren't just for athletes. They're for anyone trying to navigate life with purpose. Anyone who has faced setbacks, pressure, or uncertainty. Anyone who wants to learn how to dig in, hold form, and trust their training when the curve demands everything you've got.

I'm proud of my friend. His challenges as a young man never defined him; they only grounded him in the desire to be better, and better he became. I'm proud of this book. And I'm grateful you get to experience what so many people across the years have learned from Jiles: that even when the race feels hard, you already have what you need to finish strong.

— **Rod Barksdale**

In Loving Memory of Ursula Martin

My beloved daughter, Ursula; my oldest, my fellow track athlete, and one of the brightest souls I have ever known.

You followed in my footsteps as a track athlete, carrying the same determination, heart, and fire that shaped my own journey. Even from a distance, watching you grow into a strong, talented young woman filled me with pride I still feel today. And the times I did have the privilege to coach you, moments that were all too few, were among the sweetest of my life. In those glimpses of shared purpose, I saw the very best of both of us.

You were kind. You were a leader. You inspired everyone around you with your strength, your grace, and your unwavering spirit. Though you are no longer here, your light continues to guide me every day.

This book is for you, Ursula; my daughter, my inspiration, my forever reminder of what it truly means to run with heart.

Dad

Introduction: Life's Ultimate Race

When I coached high school track at a small school, I used to repeat the same line at nearly every practice:

"The 400 meters is the most important race."

At first, it was just something I said out of habit. But as the season went on, the athletes began to notice.

One afternoon after practice, a few of them gathered around me, sweat still glistening on their faces.

"Coach," one of them asked, "why do you always say that?"

I smiled, because I'd been waiting for that question. "Because," I said, "the 400 meters isn't just a race, it's a metaphor for life."

The 400 is unique. At your level, it's not a flat-out sprint like the 100, where raw speed wins. And it's not a long-distance grind, where endurance alone carries you home. The 400 demands balance—speed, strategy, endurance, and mental toughness. It tests every part of an athlete. Just like life does.

That day, I motioned for the team to follow me around the track. At each section, I stopped and showed them how the race mirrors the human journey.

The Starting Blocks: Ages 0–20: The first 100 meters the explosive start represents the foundation of life. Childhood, adolescence, and young adulthood. It's where we learn form, discipline, and self-belief. Every decision made in this stretch builds the rhythm for what's ahead. The false starts, the stumbles, the moments we find our stride, all of it matters.

The Backstretch: Ages 21–40: The next straightaway is where the pace evens out and the real work begins. It's early adulthood—the grind years—career building, family, financial pressure, and identity. It's where rhythm becomes more important than raw energy. Some start too fast and burn out. Others find a pace they can sustain. This is where the runners of life begin to separate—those who panic versus those who trust their preparation.

The Second Curve: Ages 41–60: The curve tests form and focus. It's the phase of life where experience meets endurance. We've learned the rhythm, but now the race bends. Our bodies slow, priorities shift, and our perspective widens. This is where we begin to build legacy—to lead, mentor, and stabilize. It's also where the fatigue of responsibility meets the wisdom of experience. Those who've learned to adjust—to run smarter, not harder—find their second wind here.

The Final Straightaway: Ages 61+: Then comes the last 100 meters—the home stretch. Fatigue sets in, but so does clarity. Every lesson, every mistake, every ounce of training culminates here. Some fade, while others dig deep, finishing not just with strength but with grace. The crowd might not see the years of effort behind that final push, but the runner feels it. Every stride is a memory. Every breath, a victory.

As I spoke that day, something shifted in my athletes. Some nodded quietly. Others stared down the track, their faces thoughtful. They realized that I wasn't just talking about running—I was talking about living.

That practice wasn't about split times or conditioning. It was about perspective. It was about helping them understand that life, like the 400, demands everything from you—and then asks for a little more.

Now, I want to share that same lesson with you.

Life is a race we all run, whether we realize it or not. Some people jog through it, content just to finish. Others charge too fast, only to fade before the end. But those who understand the rhythm—the ones who prepare, endure, and adapt—are the ones who truly win.

This book is about running your 400-meter race the right way.

It's about the preparation, the perseverance, and the purpose required to finish strong.

So, step onto the track with me.

Take your mark.

The race is about to begin.

Part I
The Start (0–20 Years): Acceleration and Discovery

Chapter 1

On Your Marks

Laying the Foundation

Key Learnings:

- The first 100 meters of life, our childhood and adolescence, establish the rhythm for everything that follows.
- Family, community, and early environments shape our worldview and self-belief long before we recognize it.
- Education and discipline are the twin forces that turn potential into performance.
- Adversity is not an interruption in our race; it is training for endurance.
- The foundation of a fulfilled life begins with awareness: learning who we are, where we come from, and how we respond to struggle.

Introduction: The Work Before the Curve

Every race begins long before the gun starts. The preparation happens in quiet mornings, on empty tracks, and in unseen hours of effort.

The first 100 meters of life are like that, the stretch where you learn discipline, build habits, and decide what kind of person you'll be when fatigue sets in later.

Some people sprint early, burn out, and fade before the curve. Others never leave the blocks, content to stand in the shade while time moves on. The wise few put in steady, deliberate effort, knowing that what they build now will carry them through the toughest turns ahead.

It's a truth as old as work itself.

Story: The Two Men and the Tree

One summer afternoon, two men sat beneath a wide oak tree at the edge of a field.

The first man, Ethan, leaned back against the trunk, eyes half closed, enjoying the shade. The other, Caleb, wiped the sweat from his brow and leaned on his hoe.

"Why do you work so hard in this heat?" Ethan asked, watching the man return to plowing. "The sun will still rise tomorrow whether you toil or not."

Caleb smiled faintly. "That's true," he said, "but tomorrow's sun doesn't promise comfort to the man who does nothing today."

Ethan chuckled. "You're missing the beauty of life, my friend. Look at this tree, strong, full of shade, and it does no work at all."

Caleb looked up at the branches swaying above them. "The tree worked once," he said. "It pushed through the soil, reached for the light, and drank every drop of rain it could. Now it rests because it grew strong enough to stand on its own."

Ethan waved him off and stretched out in the grass. Caleb returned to his field, cutting wood and planting crops until the light began to fade.

Winter came early that year.

The wind cut through the valley like knives, and the fields lay silent under snow.

Ethan huddled in a shallow cave, wrapped in thin blankets. His stomach groaned, and the cold gnawed at his bones. He thought of the long summer days he spent resting, laughing at Caleb's labor.

One night, desperate for warmth, he stumbled through the snow and saw a faint glow in the distance. It was Caleb's cabin, solid, warm, and alive with the crackle of fire. Smoke rose from the chimney, carrying the smell of stew and roasted meat.

Caleb opened the door and saw his old friend trembling in the cold. Without a word, he brought him inside, wrapped him in a blanket, and handed him a bowl of food.

Ethan looked around the cabin, stacked firewood, dried herbs hanging from the ceiling, jars of grain lined neatly on the shelves.

"You were right," Ethan whispered. "I thought I was living while you worked, but now I see I was only wasting time."

Caleb stirred the pot and smiled gently. "We all live by the seeds we plant," he said. "Some sow early and harvest peace later. Others rest early and harvest regret."

Outside, the wind howled, but inside the cabin, the fire burned bright, a reward for the man who had prepared for winter long before it came.

Reflection: The Discipline Dividend

The two men under the tree are every generation's story: the one who prepares and the one who waits. In the early seasons of life, effort feels optional because the consequences are far away. But the "field" of your youth is where you build your strength, learn endurance, and create habits that sustain you later.

The race of life is long, and it punishes those who coast early. Every lap has its own work, but the hardest labor, the cutting, planting, and training, belongs to the beginning. Those who push through the heat of the day can rest later in warmth. Those who rest too early find themselves cold when winter comes.

When you're young, physically, mentally, or spiritually, work like Caleb did. Build your cabin before the snow. Train before the race. Learn when no one's watching. Because in the sunset of life, you'll be grateful you did.

The first 100 meters aren't about speed; they're about foundation. Run them with purpose, and the curve will carry you home.

The Metaphor of the Start

As a coach, I used to tell my athletes that the 400-meter race was the most honest race ever invented. You can't fake your way through it. It's too long to sprint and too short to pace. The race demands balance, speed, endurance, and strategy, and those same demands define life itself.

I remember one late-afternoon practice on a dusty high school track, where I gathered my runners around the starting line. "This," I said, pointing at the blocks, "is where it all begins. Everything you've done up to this point has prepared you for this moment. But how you start will influence how you finish."

A student raised his hand. "Coach, why are you so obsessed with the 400?"

I laughed. "Because this race," I said, "is life." The start isn't about being perfect, it's about learning form. Everyone leaves the blocks differently, but how you handle your first 100 meters tells the story of how you'll handle the next 300."

That day, I watched their faces shift from amusement to understanding. They started to see what I saw: that the track is a metaphor for everything childhood, struggle, discovery, and the beginning of purpose. The start of the race mirrors our first twenty years, the time when our foundation is being poured, often unevenly, but always with possibility.

Family and Environment: The First Lane

Family is the first institution we ever join, and for better or worse, it defines the emotional rhythm of our early life. Psychologist John Bowlby's (1982) attachment theory explains how early caregiver relationships serve as a blueprint for all future bonds. Children who experience secure attachments are more likely to develop confidence and empathy, while inconsistent or neglectful environments often lead to anxiety, withdrawal, or aggression (Sroufe, 2005).

For me, those theories weren't abstract; they were lived reality. I grew up in a single-parent household with six children. My mother worked two jobs, sometimes three, to keep us afloat. We didn't have much, but we had her willpower. She taught us that love and discipline were not opposites. There were nights when the refrigerator held little more than leftovers and determination, but she found a way to make that enough.

Research backs what experience teaches: scarcity can sharpen focus. Children raised in lower socioeconomic environments often develop advanced coping mechanisms, a concept psychologists call "adaptive calibration" (Frankenhuis & de Weerth, 2013). In simple terms, hardship trains resourcefulness. Yet poverty also amplifies stress and limits opportunity, producing a paradox that those who survive it often become strong, but at a cost (Evans & Kim, 2013).

Looking back, my mother was both coach and example. She never used the language of psychology, but she modeled it daily: perseverance, boundaries, grit. She taught us that we didn't need to run someone else's race, we just needed to stay in our lane.

Education and Discipline: Building the Form

In a race, form matters. A sloppy start wastes energy, tight shoulders slow momentum. The same is true in life. Education and discipline are how we refine form, learn rhythm, and translate raw ability into mastery.

Bronfenbrenner's (1979) ecological systems theory reminds us that learning doesn't happen in isolation; it's influenced by the environment: families, schools, peers, and communities. In that sense, education is not just about books and classrooms; it's about the ecosystem that either nurtures or neglects curiosity.

When I was young, our school district didn't have the resources that wealthier neighborhoods had. We had hand-me-down textbooks and outdated materials. A guidance counselor once told me, "Kids like you should focus on getting a trade, not college." It wasn't cruelty, it was conditioning. Yet, as researcher Angela Duckworth (2016) found, grit, defined as perseverance and passion for long-term goals, often outweighs talent in predicting success. I decided that if grit could bridge the gap, I'd build my bridge one step at a time.

Discipline became my form. I woke up early to train, studied when my friends were out, and worked odd jobs to afford application fees. Each repetition, whether on the track or in the classroom, was a small act of rebellion against statistics. The discipline that shaped my legs also shaped my mind.

Psychologist Carol Dweck's (2006) work on growth mindset supports this connection. When students believe that effort leads to improvement, rather than seeing ability as fixed, they develop persistence in the face of challenges. That belief system becomes a psychological muscle, one that strengthens with use and defines how we respond to setbacks later in life.

In short, education gives you the map. Discipline teaches you how to read it while running at full speed.

Adversity and Resilience: Training Under Pressure

No athlete grows stronger without resistance. The same is true of people. Adversity forces adaptation, and how we respond to it often determines our trajectory.

I remember standing on the track one evening, the wind cutting across the lanes, watching a student false-start again. He dropped his head in frustration. "Coach, I can't get it right," he said. I told him what I needed to hear at his age: "You're not failing. You're training under pressure."

Developmental psychologist Ann Masten (2001) calls resilience "ordinary magic." It's the ability to recover, recalibrate, and continue despite difficulty. Research shows that resilience is not a trait we're born with; it's a skill we build through exposure to manageable stress, supportive relationships, and purpose (Masten, 2014).

As a kid, my adversity came in the form of instability and low expectations. Teachers didn't always see potential in students who looked like me. We were often measured by the problems around us instead of the possibilities within us. But I found refuge in athletics, a place where effort and performance spoke louder than stereotypes. Sports provided feedback: if you practiced, you improved; if you slacked, you fell behind. That kind of meritocracy can be liberating for a young mind searching for fairness in an unfair world.

Adversity, I learned, doesn't stop the race. It teaches you how to breathe when you're tired.

Ambition and Vision: Seeing Beyond the Blocks

Dreaming is a skill, too. For some, ambition is inherited, a natural extension of opportunity. For others, it must be built from scratch.

Goal-setting theory suggests that specific, challenging goals improve performance by providing clarity and motivation (Locke & Latham, 2002). My goal was simple: college. Not because it guaranteed success, but because it symbolized escape. It represented movement a lane forward.

Sociologist Annette Lareau (2011) described how middle-class families practice "concerted cultivation," intentionally exposing children to enriching experiences and structured learning. In contrast, working-class families often emphasize independence and resilience, producing children with strong self-reliance but fewer institutional advantages. I saw that contrast firsthand. My peers from more stable backgrounds seemed to run smoother races, but my hunger to catch them became my motivation.

Ambition became the spark; education and discipline were the fuel. Over time, I learned that success isn't a sprint to wealth or status. It's alignment living in a way that reflects who you are and what you value.

And that understanding begins early, in those first 100 meters of life when your stride is forming and your lungs are still learning rhythm.

The Influence of Mentors: Passing the Baton

If family gives you the lane and education gives you the form, mentors teach you how to use them both.

During high school, my coach, Curtis Seymore, became that figure for me. He saw potential where I saw limits. He pushed, challenged, and at times frustrated me but he never gave up. Under his guidance, the race became more than a sport. It became a language of self-discovery.

Research validates what experience proves: mentoring relationships are protective factors against poverty, delinquency, and school dropout (DuBois et al., 2002). A trusted mentor can shift a student's trajectory simply by modeling possibility. They pass the baton not of power, but of perspective.

Later, at the University of Arizona, Coach Willie Williams expanded that lesson. He taught that running fast mattered less than running smart, that pacing, strategy, and form would outlast any temporary burst of speed. His wisdom translates far beyond the track: consistency beats chaos; preparation beats panic.

Every successful person carries invisible batons handed down from those who believed in them. The start of life isn't about running alone; it's about recognizing who's in your relay.

Personal Reflections

When I think back on my early years, I see them as a race against invisibility. There were days when I felt unseen, running hard with no applause in sight. But that's what the first 100 meters often are, a lonely stretch where belief must come from within.

My mother's quiet endurance was my first lesson in resilience. My coaches gave me language for it. Together, they taught me that you can't always control where you start, but you can control how you respond.

I learned that success is built, not inherited. Every morning run before school; every late-night studying under a dim lamp; every moment spent refusing to quit was a step toward redefining my lane. I wasn't just running toward something; I was running from the idea that circumstance defines destiny.

Now, as an adult, when I mentor young people facing the same storms I did, I tell them what I wish someone had told me at fifteen: You are not behind. You are in your first 100 meters. Learn your form, keep your focus, and remember the curve is coming, but you'll be ready.

Conclusion

The first 100 meters of life are about acceleration, not arrival. They are where we build resilience, form identity, and learn rhythm. Mistakes are not missteps; they are practice. Whether your start was smooth or shaky, it is only the beginning. What matters most is not where you begin, but how you adjust, how you learn, and how you keep running.

References

Bowlby, J. (1982). Attachment and loss: Vol. 1. Attachment (2nd ed.). Basic Books.

Bronfenbrenner, U. (1979). The ecology of human development. Harvard University Press.

Duckworth, A. L. (2016). Grit: The power of passion and perseverance. Scribner.

Dweck, C. S. (2006). Mindset: The new psychology of success. Random House.

DuBois, D. L., Holloway, B. E., Valentine, J. C., & Cooper, H. (2002). Effectiveness of mentoring programs for youth: A meta-analytic review. American Journal of Community Psychology, 30(2), 157–197.

Evans, G. W., & Kim, P. (2013). Childhood poverty, chronic stress, self-regulation, and coping. Child Development Perspectives, 7(1), 43–48.

Frankenhuis, W. E., & de Weerth, C. (2013). Does early-life exposure to stress shape or impair cognition? Current Directions in Psychological Science, 22(5), 407–412.

Lareau, A. (2011). Unequal childhoods: Class, race, and family life (2nd ed.). University of California Press.

Locke, E. A., & Latham, G. P. (2002). Building a practically useful theory of goal setting and task motivation: A 35-year odyssey. American Psychologist, 57(9), 705–717.

Masten, A. S. (2001). Ordinary magic: Resilience processes in development. American Psychologist, 56(3), 227–238.

Masten, A. S. (2014). Ordinary magic: Resilience in development. Guilford Press.

Sroufe, L. A. (2005). Attachment and development: A prospective, longitudinal study from birth to adulthood. Attachment & Human Development, 7(4), 349–367.

Chapter 2

Set

Learning the Fundamentals

Key Learnings

- The "set" phase of life adolescence and early adulthood is where alignment happens between potential and purpose.
- Social environments, mentors, and education shape how we learn to handle responsibility and pressure.
- Self-awareness, identity, and discipline become the foundation for long-term success.
- Early failures, when reframed, teach persistence and adaptability.
- Preparation is not about perfection it's about getting ready to move with intent when life's gun goes off.

Introduction: The Stillness Before the Sprint

There's a unique kind of silence that settles over a track just before the starter's pistol fires. Every runner is coiled in the blocks, muscles taut, heart racing. The command "Set!" isn't about movement; it's about readiness. It's the pause before purpose, the moment when focus meets form.

That moment mirrors adolescence and young adulthood. You're not running yet, but everything you're doing - the lessons, friendships, heartbreaks, and habits - is shaping how you'll leave the blocks. I used to tell my athletes that races are rarely won at the start, but they're often lost there. You can have raw talent, but if you don't learn timing, balance, and control, you'll stumble before you even hit stride.

Life's "set" stage, roughly ages 10 to 20, isn't about arrival; it's about alignment. It's the time when we learn who we are, where we fit, and how we respond to pressure. These are the years where small decisions, such as how we study, who we listen to, and who we become, set the pace for everything that follows.

The Power of School and Social Influence

Bronfenbrenner's (1979) ecological systems theory reminds us that human development is never isolated; it's relational. Our growth depends on overlapping circles of influence: family, school, community, and society. During adolescence, the circle widens dramatically. Friends begin to matter more, mentors shape direction, and belonging becomes both a need and a test.

Friendships in adolescence serve as the first laboratory for empathy and trust. They teach negotiation, forgiveness, and the limits of loyalty (Hartup, 1996). For me, those relationships were both a lifeline and a lesson. Some friends pushed me forward, while others tempted me off the track entirely. I learned early that not everyone in your lane is running your race.

School was no less complicated. The classrooms were crowded, resources thin, and expectations uneven. But even in underfunded schools, great teachers can become turning points. One teacher, Ms. Hernandez, once told me, "You don't need to be the smartest. Just don't stop trying." It wasn't poetry, but it was truth. Studies show that even one supportive teacher relationship can significantly boost a student's long-term academic motivation (Roorda et al., 2011).

Mentors bridge the gap between what we see and what we believe is possible. My high school coach, the same one who taught me how to explode out of the blocks, also taught me how to think under pressure. He'd say, "Anyone can run fast when it's easy. Show me how you run tired." Those words echoed far beyond the track.

Research supports what lived experience confirms: sustained mentorship, whether through formal programs or organic relationships, builds resilience and goal orientation (Rhodes, 2005; DuBois et al., 2002). Good mentors don't just show you the lane, they help you believe you belong in it.

Identity and the Search for Direction

Erik Erikson (1968) described adolescence as the stage of identity versus role confusion, the psychological tug-of-war between who we are and who others expect us to be. Every teenager, in one way or another, asks the same question: "Who am I becoming?"

For me, that question came early. I knew I didn't fit the narrow definitions that my environment tried to assign me. Some saw a promising athlete; others saw another kid from a rough neighborhood destined to fade. Neither label felt complete. It wasn't until college that I realized identity isn't something you find, it's something you build, one decision at a time.

Cognitive scientists note that adolescence is a period of massive brain restructuring, particularly in the prefrontal cortex, which governs impulse control and decision-making (Casey et al., 2008). That biological truth helps explain why young people often make bold, sometimes reckless, choices; it's part of the wiring. But it also highlights why consistent guidance during this period is essential.

Participation in structured activities such as sports, clubs, and community service has been shown to foster leadership, self-regulation, and a sense of purpose (Mahoney et al., 2005). These environments don't just occupy time; they shape character. They teach young people to navigate complexity, collaborate with others, and develop the discipline of showing up, skills that carry far beyond adolescence.

Adolescence is less about discovering a single identity and more about learning how to stay grounded amid competing ones. It's about deciding which voices to trust and when to listen to your own.

Responsibility: The First Weight You Carry

When you first step into the "set" position, your body holds tension and an invisible weight, preparing you to move. Responsibility feels the same way. It's pressure that prepares us.

Taking on responsibility early, whether through chores, jobs, or leadership roles, creates a sense of agency. Adolescents who are trusted with real, age-appropriate responsibilities develop stronger confidence and self-regulation later in life (Larson et al., 1996). For me, responsibility wasn't optional; it was survival.

By high school, I was balancing academics, athletics, and part-time work. Each task, each obligation, was a muscle that strengthened self-discipline. I didn't always appreciate it then, but now I see that responsibility was teaching me the physics of life: you can't move forward without friction.

Research by Deci and Ryan (2000) on self-determination theory shows that autonomy, choosing responsibility rather than avoiding it, creates intrinsic motivation. When we own our duties, they stop being burdens and start becoming proof that we're capable.

Responsibility, like training, doesn't remove difficulty; it builds capacity to carry it.

Learning to Handle Pressure

Every athlete eventually faces pressure; the kind that makes your chest tighten and your thoughts race. For young people, pressure comes in many forms: academic expectations, social judgment, or the silent war between self-worth and self-doubt.

I remember the first time I choked in competition. It was a regional meet. The crowd was loud, the stakes high. I false-started not once, but twice. I felt the weight of eyes on me, the disappointment of my team. Afterward, my coach pulled me aside and said quietly, "Pressure doesn't create weakness; it exposes where you need strength."

He was right. I began studying how elite performers manage stress. Breathing techniques, visualization, and mental rehearsal, all strategies used by athletes, are equally valuable in daily life. Research supports this: mindfulness and cognitive reframing reduce anxiety and enhance performance across domains (Chiesa & Serretti, 2009; Compas et al., 2001).

Adolescence teaches this lesson early. You learn that perfection isn't the goal, control is. Not control over the world, but over yourself. Those who master that balance go on to handle life's "big races" with composure.

Failure and Growth

Failure is not disqualification; it's data. Every false start, every missed opportunity, every loss contains information about what to fix.

As Carol Dweck (2006) argues, a growth mindset, believing that ability can improve through effort, transforms failure from a verdict into a tool. That mindset isn't just for students; it's for life. I learned that lesson the hard way.

During my junior year, I applied for a summer leadership program and didn't get in. I was crushed. I thought I wasn't smart enough or connected enough. But that rejection forced me to create my own opportunities to train harder, network better, and prepare more thoroughly the next time. The following year, I was accepted.

In retrospect, I see how every "no" prepared me for bigger "yeses." Research on resilience confirms that exposure to moderate stress enhances adaptability, a phenomenon psychologists call "stress inoculation" (Seery, 2011). Simply put: a little struggle strengthens your stride.

Failure doesn't define your race. It defines your readiness.

Personal Reflections

When I think about my "set" years, I remember how uncertain everything felt. I was ready to move but unsure where to go. I had drive without direction, and that mix of ambition and fear defined much of my teenage life.

The truth is, I didn't have a roadmap. What I had was momentum, fueled by my mother's voice, my coaches' lessons, and the quiet conviction that life had to be bigger than my circumstances. I learned to take pride in the preparation, not just the performance.

Every challenge during those years of academic struggles, financial stress, or moments of doubt wasn't a setback; it was calibration. I was learning how to hold pressure without breaking, how to trust my form when the world shouted distractions.

Now, when I mentor young people standing at their own starting lines, I tell them: Don't rush the set. The stillness you feel right now isn't wasted time; it's power building up. The patience you practice now will become your speed later. The alignment you find now will carry you through every curve.

Conclusion

The "set" phase of life isn't glamorous, but it's critical. It's the stage where timing, confidence, and preparation converge. The friends you choose, the lessons you embrace, and the habits you build become the foundation of your form.

In the race of life, we all crouch at the line at some point waiting for the gun, unsure if we're ready. The truth is, no one ever feels fully ready. But those who take the time to prepare, to align their focus and form, explode into the next phase with purpose.

Preparation doesn't guarantee an easy race, but it ensures you'll run it with strength and intention.

References

Bronfenbrenner, U. (1979). The ecology of human development. Harvard University Press.

Casey, B. J., Getz, S., & Galvan, A. (2008). The adolescent brain. Developmental Review, 28(1), 62–77.

Chiesa, A., & Serretti, A. (2009). Mindfulness-based stress reduction for stress management: A meta-analysis. Journal of Alternative and Complementary Medicine, 15(5), 593–600.

Compas, B. E., Connor-Smith, J. K., Saltzman, H., Thomsen, A. H., & Wadsworth, M. E. (2001). Coping with stress during childhood and adolescence. Psychological Bulletin, 127(1), 87–127.

Deci, E. L., & Ryan, R. M. (2000). The "what" and "why" of goal pursuits: Human needs and the self-determination of behavior. Psychological Inquiry, 11(4), 227–268.

Dweck, C. S. (2006). Mindset: The new psychology of success. Random House.

DuBois, D. L., Holloway, B. E., Valentine, J. C., & Cooper, H. (2002). Effectiveness of mentoring programs for youth: A meta-analytic review. American Journal of Community Psychology, 30(2), 157–197.

Erikson, E. H. (1968). Identity: Youth and crisis. W. W. Norton & Company.

Hartup, W. W. (1996). The company they keep: Friendships and their developmental significance. Child Development, 67(1), 1–13.

Larson, R. W., & Verma, S. (1999). How children and adolescents spend time across the world: Work, play, and developmental opportunities. Psychological Bulletin, 125(6), 701–736.

Mahoney, J. L., Larson, R. W., & Eccles, J. S. (2005). Organized activities as contexts of development: Extracurricular activities, after-school, and community programs. Psychology Press.

Rhodes, J. E. (2005). A model of youth mentoring. The Journal of Community Psychology, 33(6), 691–707.

Roorda, D. L., Koomen, H. M., Spilt, J. L., & Oort, F. J. (2011). The influence of affective teacher–student relationships on students' school engagement and achievement: A meta-analytic approach. Review of Educational Research, 81(4), 493–529.

Seery, M. D. (2011). Resilience: A silver lining to experiencing adverse life events? Current Directions in Psychological Science, 20(6), 390–394.

Chapter 3

Go!

The First Stride into Independence

Key Learnings:

- Independence begins the moment we move from expectation to ownership.
- Early adulthood is less about stability and more about experimentation, failure, and adaptation.
- Purpose requires both motion and reflection; speed without direction leads to burnout.
- Financial, emotional, and social independence grow at different rates and require different kinds of discipline.
- The first stride into adulthood is rarely perfect, but it defines how we recover, recalibrate, and run forward.

Introduction: The Gun Goes Off

There's nothing quite like the sound of a starting gun. It's loud, sudden, and impossible to ignore. One second you're still, balanced on the blocks, heart hammering in your chest; the next, you're in motion, knees driving, arms swinging, lungs burning.

That moment mirrors early adulthood. After years of preparation, schooling, advice, and structure, life suddenly fires its gun. You're expected to know where you're going, how to move, and what pace to set, even though no one ever taught you how to breathe once you're on your own.

I still remember that feeling when I left home for the first time. The freedom was thrilling, but it came with weight: bills, responsibilities, choices. The air felt different. I'd gone from being coached to coaching myself, and there was no whistle to tell me when to rest. The race had officially begun.

The first stride of independence is where many stumble, not from lack of effort, but from lack of rhythm. It's the stage of learning how to manage momentum: too slow, and life passes you by; too fast, and you lose your form.

Learning to Stand Alone

Independence isn't just about moving out of your parents' house; it's about developing the capacity to self-direct. Psychologists define this as "autonomous functioning," where decisions and behaviors are guided by internal values rather than external pressures (Ryan & Deci, 2017).

For many young adults, the early twenties bring what sociologist Jeffrey Arnett (2000) called emerging adulthood, a developmental phase marked by exploration, instability, and identity formation.

It's a period when people are both independent and dependent, confident and uncertain.

When I first started working full-time, I realized how little I understood about life beyond the classroom. Managing money, setting boundaries, balancing exhaustion and ambition, these weren't subjects anyone taught. The real test wasn't professional; it was personal. Could I sustain motivation when no one was grading me?

Research shows that early independence can predict future well-being, but only when supported by meaningful relationships (Allen et al., 2014). Too much isolation leads to burnout, too much dependence delays growth. Balance, as in running, is everything.

In your twenties, you learn that freedom without discipline is chaos and discipline without purpose is prison.

The Illusion of Arrival

When you're young, you're told that independence is the finish line that once you "make it" (a job, an apartment, a relationship), life will smooth out. But the truth is, independence is the starting line of self-definition.

I remember getting my first real paycheck and feeling invincible until rent, groceries, and car insurance took it back. That's when I learned the first unwritten rule of adulthood: independence comes with invoices.

Financial independence often arrives last. Studies show that many young adults remain financially tied to their parents well into their twenties (Fry, 2020). But beyond money, there's emotional and moral independence, the ability to make choices without needing validation.

That kind of freedom takes courage. As Erich Fromm (1941) wrote in Escape from Freedom, people often flee from true independence because it demands responsibility. It's easier to follow directions than to design a life.

I've seen many talented people stall because they confuse motion with progress. They ran hard but without direction, chasing titles, possessions, or approval. Without a clear sense of purpose, speed becomes exhaustion disguised as achievement.

Finding Rhythm: The Balance Between Hustle and Rest

In the 400-meter race, runners often go out too fast. The adrenaline from the start makes restraint feel like weakness. But experienced runners know that what you save in the first 100 meters, you spend wisely in the last 100.

Early adulthood is no different. The temptation to over-commit to chase every goal at once can lead to burnout. Sociologists call this "time famine," a constant sense that there's never enough time to do or be enough (Roxburgh, 2004).

I've lived through that famine. Early in my career, I said yes to everything, such as projects, overtime, travel, and committees. I was sprinting without a strategy. My days blurred into months until one afternoon, sitting in traffic, I realized I couldn't remember the last time I'd laughed without checking the clock.

That moment forced a shift. I began studying balance the same way I'd studied speed. Research on psychological well-being confirms that rest, mindfulness, and social connection are not luxuries; they're essential to sustainable performance (Brown & Ryan, 2003; Killingsworth & Gilbert, 2010).

I learned that running the curve of life isn't about how fast you move, but how intentionally you breathe. Rest isn't retreat; it's rhythm.

Relationships and Connection

As independence grows, relationships take on new meaning. No longer shaped by proximity like school or, they become intentional. You choose who to spend your time with, and those choices shape your trajectory.

Research shows that adults who cultivate strong social bonds experience better mental health, resilience, and longevity (Holt-Lunstad et al., 2010). Yet, in a culture that glorifies self-reliance, many confuse independence with isolation.

I've seen people, myself included, equate strength with solitude. But real independence isn't doing everything alone; it's knowing when to ask for help. Relationships are the teammates in our individual races. Some will pace you, some will challenge you, and a few will trip you, but each teaches something about endurance.

In my twenties, I learned that love and loyalty are not automatic. They require communication, humility, and shared effort. Whether romantic or platonic, relationships become the mirrors that reveal our strengths and blind spots.

Connection doesn't slow you down; it gives you stamina for the long run.

The Economics of Independence

Money has a way of turning philosophy into reality. The first time I balanced a checkbook (or tried to), I realized that independence without financial literacy is just expensive freedom.

Studies show that financial stress is one of the top predictors of anxiety among young adults (Serido et al., 2010). Economic independence is more than income; it's control, awareness, and planning. Learning to budget, save, and invest is like learning pacing in a race. Spend too fast early, and you're gasping later.

For me, that meant learning humility. I didn't grow up with financial guidance, so I made plenty of mistakes with credit cards, impulsive purchases, and overextending myself to look successful. It took time to understand that wealth isn't what you show; it's what you manage.

I started reading about personal finance, investing, and long-term planning. The principles were simple but profound: pay yourself first, live below your means, invest in learning. Those lessons didn't just improve my bank account; they built patience.

Financial independence taught me the same truth the track always did: that consistency beats intensity.

Resilience in Transition

The first years on your own test your resilience in ways no classroom can prepare you for. Suddenly, you're responsible for your mistakes. There's no safety net, no late pass, no parent-teacher conference.

But that's where true growth happens. As psychologist Albert Bandura (1997) described, self-efficacy is the belief in your ability to succeed, built not from ease but from overcoming difficulty.

Each bill paid, conflict resolved, and decision made adds to your internal confidence.

Life after the starting gun is full of unknowns like job rejections, heartbreaks, and financial shortfalls, but these experiences are not detours; they're conditioning. They develop the mental endurance required for the next curve.

Every runner knows that by the time you hit your stride, your muscles are burning, but your focus sharpens. Independence works the same way. It hurts before it harmonizes.

Personal Reflections

When I look back at my twenties, I see a young man sprinting with a mixture of fear and faith. I was eager to prove to myself that hard work could overcome any starting position. But in that eagerness, I often ran too fast, chasing validation instead of purpose.

There were moments I confused busyness for progress. I wore exhaustion like a badge of honor, believing that slowing down meant losing. It took several stumbles, financial setbacks, failed relationships, and burnout to realize that independence isn't speed; it's self-command.

What I remember most are the quiet nights in small apartments, wondering if I was on the right path. Those doubts were the sound of growth. They forced me to think critically, to redefine success not by status, but by steadiness.

Now, when I mentor younger professionals, I tell them: Go but don't go blind. Life will demand movement, but it will also test your control. Independence is not the absence of guidance; it's the maturity to apply what you've learned when no one's watching.

Conclusion

The "go" phase of life is exhilarating and exhausting. It's where preparation meets reality and idealism collides with responsibility. Mistakes are inevitable, but they're also instructive.

Like the first 100 meters of the 400, this phase sets rhythm and tone. You'll stumble, recover, adjust your stride, but with each step, you'll grow into your independence. The key is not to outrun your learning. Pace yourself, stay grounded, and remember: the real race isn't against others, it's against your own impatience.

References

Allen, J. P., Chango, J., Szwedo, D., Schad, M., & Marston, E. (2014). Predictors of susceptibility to peer influence regarding substance use in adolescence. Child Development, 85(1), 337–350.

Arnett, J. J. (2000). Emerging adulthood: A theory of development from the late teens through the twenties. American Psychologist, 55(5), 469–480.

Bandura, A. (1997). Self-efficacy: The exercise of control. W. H. Freeman and Company.

Brown, K. W., & Ryan, R. M. (2003). The benefits of being present: Mindfulness and its role in psychological well-being. Journal of Personality and Social Psychology, 84(4), 822–848.

Fromm, E. (1941). Escape from freedom. Farrar & Rinehart.

Fry, R. (2020). A rising share of young adults in the U.S. are living with their parents. Pew Research Center.

Holt-Lunstad, J., Smith, T. B., & Layton, J. B. (2010). Social relationships and mortality risk: A meta-analytic review. PLoS Medicine, 7(7), e1000316.

Killingsworth, M. A., & Gilbert, D. T. (2010). A wandering mind is an unhappy mind. Science, 330(6006), 932.

Roxburgh, S. (2004). "There just aren't enough hours in the day": The mental health consequences of time pressure. Journal of Health and Social Behavior, 45(2), 115–131.

Ryan, R. M., & Deci, E. L. (2017). Self-determination theory: Basic psychological needs in motivation, development, and wellness. Guilford Press.

Serido, J., Shim, S., Mishra, A., & Tang, C. (2010). Financial parenting, financial coping behaviors, and well-being of emerging adults. Journal of Family and Economic Issues, 31(4), 469–479.

Part II

The Backstretch (Ages 21–40)

Drive and Direction

Chapter 4 Finding Your Rhythm

Establishing Stability

Key Learnings:

- After the explosive start of early adulthood, stability comes from pacing, not speed.
- Success in your 20s and 30s depends less on talent and more on rhythm, knowing when to accelerate, when to recover, and when to pivot.
- Career growth, relationships, and self-identity stabilize when consistency replaces chaos.
- Emotional intelligence becomes as critical as ambition in sustaining long-term success.
- True rhythm isn't balance in the moment, it's harmony over time.

Introduction: The Long Stretch Ahead

In the 400-meter race, the backstretch is deceptive. It looks like freedom because of the open track and the lack of tight turns, but it's where the race begins to demand rhythm. Sprinters who went out too fast are already tightening up; those who started too slow are trying to make up ground. The ones who succeed are those who find their cadence steady, strong, and deliberate.

Life's backstretch, roughly ages 21 to 40, feels just like that. The chaos of your early twenties starts to quiet. You've learned to manage independence, maybe established a career or family, but now comes the real test: sustaining momentum. The first half of the race was about proving you could move; the second is about proving you can maintain.

This stage teaches that success is not a sprint; it's an endurance event. You begin to understand that work, relationships, and even personal growth require a rhythm you can sustain for years, not days.

Career and Calling: Pace Over Position

Early in our careers, most of us run hard for titles and validation. We equate progress with promotion, thinking that movement equals meaning. But the truth is, finding your rhythm at work is less about climbing ladders and more about defining purpose.

Research on job satisfaction shows that intrinsic motivation, such as doing work that feels meaningful, correlates far more strongly with well-being than external rewards like pay or status (Deci & Ryan, 2000). When we align values with vocation, we stop chasing approval and start chasing excellence.

In my early professional years, I chased opportunities with the intensity of a sprinter. I wanted to prove myself to show that hard work could erase doubt. But as time passed, I noticed something: I was burning energy faster than I could recover. I was working hard, but not always working right.

The lesson came through exhaustion: you can't build a long career on short bursts. Rhythm in work means understanding your strengths, managing your pace, and finding fulfillment in progress, not perfection.

Burnout, which the World Health Organization (2019) classifies as an occupational syndrome, often hits those who sprint through their professional years without rest. The antidote is intentional pacing, setting boundaries, taking breaks, and allowing space for learning instead of constant performance.

Your calling, I've learned, is not discovered in chaos. It's found in the quiet pattern of consistency.

Relationships: The Second Lap of Connection

By the time most people reach their late twenties or early thirties, their romantic, familial, and professional relationships shift from discovery to maintenance. The novelty of connection gives way to the work of communication, empathy, and compromise.

John Gottman's (1994) decades-long research on relationships revealed that successful partnerships aren't built on constant harmony but on healthy repair. Couples who can argue constructively and recover emotionally have a 94% greater chance of long-term success. The same principle applies beyond romance: whether with friends or coworkers, relationships thrive not on perfection but on emotional intelligence.

In this stretch of life, I learned that people's capacities change. Some friends grow closer, others drift. Priorities shift careers, children, health, grief. What keeps relationships strong isn't constant proximity; it's consistent presence. Even brief but genuine contact, such as calls, texts, and visits, sustains trust and emotional connection (Hall, 2019).

The backstretch of life asks you to invest in fewer but deeper relationships to run with those who match your rhythm.

Stability and the Myth of Balance

Work-life balance is a phrase often repeated, rarely achieved. In reality, balance is dynamic. No one can divide energy equally between career, family, and personal growth all the time. Stability, rather than balance, should be the goal, a rhythm that adjusts as life changes.

Psychologists Hobfoll et al. (2018) describe stability as the preservation of "resource caravans" like time, energy, relationships, and health that protect well-being under stress. The key isn't equal distribution but strategic recovery.

When I first began managing teams, I thought leadership meant constant availability. I answered emails at midnight, skipped meals, and worked through weekends. I was efficient, but not effective. It wasn't until I started prioritizing health, sleep, exercise, and quiet time that I noticed productivity and creativity improved.

Balance is a temporary equilibrium. Stability is an enduring rhythm. One survives change; the other crumbles under it.

Financial Foundations and the Long Game

If your twenties are about financial independence, your thirties are about financial intelligence. It's not just about earning, it's about managing, saving, and preparing.

Economists argue that by the mid-thirties, financial behavior habits are largely set (Lusardi & Mitchell, 2014). Those who build discipline early compound not just wealth, but peace of mind.

For me, rhythm meant setting up systems for automated savings, budgeting, and delayed gratification. I learned that money isn't the goal; it's a tool that allows you to focus on what matters. Each dollar should either earn, learn, or return, that is, grow wealth, expand knowledge, or support others.

Financial peace is rhythm expressed numerically. It's the confidence that you're running at a sustainable pace.

Self-Awareness and Emotional Rhythm

The backstretch years introduce a quieter kind of growth, the inward turn. You begin to care less about others' applause and more about your own alignment. Self-awareness, as Daniel Goleman (1995) noted in his research on emotional intelligence, is the foundation of mature leadership.

In these years, I started noticing patterns in why certain challenges kept repeating, why I reacted to stress the way I did, and why some people drained energy while others restored it. The more aware I became, the more control I had over my responses.

Research supports this evolution: mindfulness-based self-awareness increases resilience, focus, and emotional regulation (Creswell, 2017). In a world that rewards speed, reflection becomes a competitive advantage.

Finding rhythm in adulthood isn't about coasting, it's about learning the pace that allows both productivity and peace.

Personal Reflections

When I think of this phase of my life, I see a runner settling into stride. The chaos of the start is behind me, but fatigue begins to whisper. There's comfort in motion now, but also the temptation to drift to rely on momentum instead of intention.

In my thirties, I learned that rhythm isn't found in perfection. It's found in forgiveness of yourself, of others, of the pace that life demands. There were seasons when I ran too hard and seasons when I coasted, but both taught me that sustainability requires self-awareness.

There's a kind of maturity that only repetition brings the rhythm of showing up, not because it's exciting, but because it's necessary.

The rhythm of loving people consistently, even when it's inconvenient. The rhythm of faith, patience, and recovery.

I'm still learning that the measure of a good life isn't how fast you finish, but how steady you remain when the track stretches long and lonely ahead.

Conclusion

The backstretch of life is where stability is earned. It's the test of pacing, endurance, and consistency. Those who find rhythm here will carry it into the curve with confidence.

This phase isn't about glamour, it's about grounding. It's about learning to sustain your commitments, invest in your well-being, and live in a rhythm that honors both ambition and rest. The race isn't won here, but it's often lost by those who forget that the longest stretches demand the most patience.

Find your rhythm early, and the curve ahead won't break you; it will reveal your form.

References

Creswell, J. D. (2017). Mindfulness interventions. Annual Review of Psychology, 68, 491–516.

Deci, E. L., & Ryan, R. M. (2000). The "what" and "why" of goal pursuits: Human needs and the self-determination of behavior. Psychological Inquiry, 11(4), 227–268.

Goleman, D. (1995). Emotional intelligence: Why it can matter more than IQ. Bantam Books.

Gottman, J. (1994). Why marriages succeed or fail. Simon & Schuster.

Hall, J. A. (2019). How many hours does it take to make a friend? Journal of Social and Personal Relationships, 36(4), 1278–1296.

Hobfoll, S. E., Halbesleben, J., Neveu, J. P., & Westman, M. (2018). Conservation of resources in the organizational context: The reality of resources and their consequences. Annual Review of Organizational Psychology and Organizational Behavior, 5, 103–128.

Lusardi, A., & Mitchell, O. S. (2014). The economic importance of financial literacy: Theory and evidence. Journal of Economic Literature, 52(1), 5–44.

World Health Organization. (2019). Burn-out an "occupational phenomenon": International Classification of Diseases.

Chapter 5

Running in Traffic

Navigating Competition and Comparison

Key Learnings:

- Comparison is the thief of both peace and purpose; progress requires staying focused on your lane.
- Healthy competition can sharpen performance, but envy and distraction erode rhythm.
- Emotional intelligence and humility help sustain relationships in competitive environments.
- Self-worth grounded in internal values, not external validation, leads to authentic success.
- Confidence grows not from being the fastest, but from running true to your own pace and purpose.

Introduction: When the Lanes Get Crowded

By the time you hit the middle of the 400, you're surrounded. The race that started with personal focus now becomes a test of awareness. You hear footsteps to your left, breathing to your right, and instinct kicks in. You want to look, but glancing over can cost milliseconds, and in this race, milliseconds matter.

That's what competition feels like in adulthood. The world gets louder, and the temptation to measure yourself against others grows stronger. Career titles, income brackets, houses, followers, and family life become one long leaderboard if you let it.

I've been there. I've looked left and right. And every time I did, I lost form. The more I focused on other runners, the less control I had over my own stride. It took years to learn that you can run beside others without running against them.

The Psychology of Comparison

Humans are wired for comparison. Leon Festinger's (1954) social comparison theory argues that people evaluate themselves by measuring against others. It's how we gauge progress, belonging, and self-worth. But in a hyper-connected world, where everyone's highlight reel is on display, that instinct becomes toxic.

Studies show that upward comparison comparing ourselves to those we perceive as "ahead" is strongly linked to decreased self-esteem and increased anxiety (Vogel et al., 2014). In contrast, downward comparison looking at those "behind" us may bring temporary relief but doesn't inspire growth.

Social media amplifies this cycle. We compare our everyday moments to others' best ones and call it failure. The result? Burnout disguised as motivation.

Learning to quiet that noise is essential for emotional stability. As Brené Brown (2010) observed, authenticity and connection flourish only when we stop performing for approval and start living for alignment.

Healthy Competition: Iron Sharpens Iron

Competition isn't the enemy, ego is. Healthy rivalry can drive excellence when it's rooted in respect rather than insecurity.

In sports, competition is what pushes athletes to their limits. Studies show that moderate levels of competition increase intrinsic motivation and focus (Tauer & Harackiewicz, 2004). But when the desire to win becomes an obsession to outshine, it corrodes performance.

During my career, I learned that healthy competition can exist even in leadership. I admired peers who excelled in areas I lacked. Instead of resenting them, I began learning from them studying their discipline, their communication, their grace under pressure. The more I did, the more I grew.

Competition, when framed correctly, doesn't divide people; it refines them. The best competitors make everyone around them better.

Workplace Rivalry and Collaboration

Modern workplaces often blur the line between collaboration and competition. Promotions, recognition, and project ownership can turn allies into opponents. But the highest-performing teams share one thing in common: psychological safety.

Amy Edmondson (1999) defines psychological safety as the shared belief that team members can take risks, make mistakes, and share ideas without fear of humiliation. Environments that prioritize learning over judgment encourage people to perform better collectively.

When I started leading teams, I noticed that open communication transformed dynamics. Recognizing others' contributions didn't diminish mine; it amplified the group's success. Praise, I discovered, doesn't deplete; it multiplies.

True leadership isn't about running ahead of others; it's about clearing the path for them to run freely.

Ego, Humility, and Emotional Intelligence

Ego loves competition; humility loves mastery. It took me time to understand that distinction. Early in my leadership journey, I equated confidence with control. I thought being the loudest meant being the strongest. Over time, I realized real strength is quiet; it is self-control, patience, and presence.

Daniel Goleman's (1998) research on emotional intelligence identifies self-awareness, empathy, and regulation as the core of effective leadership. Those who can manage their own emotions and understand others' perspectives outperform those who lead by force.

Ego shouts. Humility listens. Ego competes for credit. Humility celebrates contribution. Ego measures worth in wins; humility measures it in wisdom.

As I learned to let go of ego, my relationships deepened and my influence grew. The irony of leadership is that you gain authority by giving it away by trusting, empowering, and lifting others.

The Cost of Distraction

When runners lose focus, even for a second, form breaks down. Shoulders tighten, breathing quickens, and rhythm falters. The same happens in life when we let comparison or competition distract us.

Cognitive psychology shows that multitasking and constant external validation deplete attention and reduce long-term performance (Ophir et al., 2009). Distraction masquerades as productivity, but it fractures progress.

I've seen people lose years chasing someone else's path, trying to keep up with neighbors, colleagues, or trends. I've done it myself. But life doesn't reward imitation; it rewards authenticity.

Once I learned to measure success by progress rather than position, I regained peace. I could appreciate others' success without feeling diminished by it.

When you stay in your lane, the noise fades, and all you hear is your own breath. That's when you know you've found your rhythm again.

Redefining Success

At this point in the race, the scoreboard becomes internal. Success stops being a public performance and becomes a private alignment. You begin asking different questions: not "Am I winning?" but "Am I well?"

Research supports this transition. Studies show that intrinsic goals, such as growth, relationships, and contribution, predict greater long-term happiness than extrinsic goals, like wealth and fame (Kasser & Ryan, 1996).

That doesn't mean ambition disappears; it matures. You start to understand that the real finish line isn't about beating others, it's about becoming yourself.

Personal Reflections

I remember a season in my career when I felt constantly surrounded. Everywhere I looked, someone seemed to be doing better. Bigger titles, nicer cars, more recognition. It felt like I was running in heavy traffic, always a half-step behind.

One day, a mentor told me, "You're losing form looking left and right. Run your race." It hit hard because I knew he was right. I was burning energy watching others instead of investing it in myself.

That conversation changed how I moved. I stopped chasing visibility and started chasing value. I learned to measure success by peace, not applause. I realized that my lane had enough room for growth, meaning, and excellence if I stayed focused on it.

Now, when I mentor others, I tell them, "Comparison kills rhythm." You can respect others' races without copying them. You can celebrate others' wins without subtracting from your own. The only real opponent is yesterday's version of you.

When I run now, whether on a track or through life, I don't look left or right anymore. I just listen to my breath and trust my pace.

Conclusion

Running in traffic is inevitable. Life crowds your lane with noise, comparison, and competition. The challenge is to maintain form to remember that your progress depends on your focus.

Healthy competition pushes us forward, but comparison pulls us backward. Stay aware of others but also stay anchored in yourself.

Success doesn't come from being ahead; it comes from being aligned.

When you stop chasing others and start refining your own rhythm, you realize something powerful: there was never traffic. Just different runners, each on their own path, chasing their own finish lines.

References

Brown, B. (2010). The gifts of imperfection. Hazelden Publishing.

Edmondson, A. (1999). Psychological safety and learning behavior in work teams. Administrative Science Quarterly, 44(2), 350–383.

Festinger, L. (1954). A theory of social comparison processes. Human Relations, 7(2), 117–140.

Goleman, D. (1998). Working with emotional intelligence. Bantam Books.

Kasser, T., & Ryan, R. M. (1996). Further examining the American dream: Differential correlates of intrinsic and extrinsic goals. Personality and Social Psychology Bulletin, 22(3), 280–287.

Ophir, E., Nass, C., & Wagner, A. D. (2009). Cognitive control in media multitaskers. Proceedings of the National Academy of Sciences, 106(37), 15583–15587.

Tauer, J. M., & Harackiewicz, J. M. (2004). The effects of cooperation and competition on intrinsic motivation and performance. Journal of Personality and Social Psychology, 86(6), 849–861.

Vogel, E. A., Rose, J. P., Roberts, L. R., & Eckles, K. (2014). Social comparison, social media, and self-esteem. Psychology of Popular Media Culture, 3(4), 206–222.

Chapter 6

The Weight of the Wind

Burnout, Doubt, and Realignment

Key Learnings:

Burnout is not a failure of strength but a signal of imbalance.

- Sustained success requires intentional rest and emotional recovery.
- Self-doubt, when examined, can become a catalyst for purpose realignment.
- Emotional and spiritual health are as vital to endurance as physical and professional performance.
- When the headwinds of life grow stronger, the goal is not to fight them but to lean into the wind with better form.

Introduction: When the Wind Turns Against You

In the 400-meter race, there's a moment halfway down the backstretch when the wind hits. It doesn't announce itself it just arrives, pressing against your chest, slowing your legs, making each stride feel heavier. Runners call it "the wall."

In life, the wall shows up, too. It's the fatigue that settles in after years of pushing, working long hours, balancing family and career, and performing under pressure. You still move, but every step feels harder. Motivation fades, passion dulls, and the once-clear finish line begins to blur.

That's burnout. Not sudden collapse, but slow erosion. It creeps in when your identity becomes intertwined with doing rather than being, when achievement replaces alignment.

I've run into that wind more than once. Each time, it forced me to relearn what the race was really about: presence, not perfection.

Understanding Burnout

Burnout is not just exhaustion; it's disconnection. Psychologist Christina Maslach (2003) defined it as a syndrome of emotional exhaustion, depersonalization, and reduced sense of accomplishment. It happens when constant effort meets diminishing meaning.

According to the World Health Organization (2019), burnout stems from chronic workplace stress that has not been successfully managed. But the phenomenon extends beyond careers; it affects parents, leaders, caregivers, and creators.

Research shows that individuals with high conscientiousness and drive, those most committed to excellence, are paradoxically the most vulnerable (Leiter & Maslach, 2009). The very traits that fuel achievement can become liabilities when left unchecked.

In my own life, burnout crept in quietly. It didn't arrive as collapse, but as numbness. I'd wake up, perform the motions, lead meetings, deliver results, and feel nothing. I had rhythm, but no resonance.

What I've learned is that burnout isn't weakness; it's data. It's the body and soul saying something is out of alignment.

The Myth of Endless Energy

We live in a culture that worships endurance and confuses rest with laziness. The idea of "grind culture" suggests that success requires relentless motion, as if fatigue were a moral failing. But every athlete knows recovery is part of training.

Research on rest and performance supports this truth. Downtime improves creativity, problem-solving, and emotional regulation (Kuhnel et al., 2017). In fact, sleep deprivation alone can impair cognitive function as much as alcohol intoxication (Walker, 2017).

During one particularly demanding year, I led multiple projects while mentoring new staff and traveling weekly. I told myself I was fine after all; I was delivering results. But inside, I was running on fumes. My focus narrowed, my patience thinned, and small frustrations became overwhelming.

Eventually, I took a week off. I didn't realize how deeply I'd crashed until the silence of rest felt foreign. It wasn't weakness, but rather withdrawal from overextension.

That week changed me. I learned that real endurance comes not from resisting fatigue but from respecting recovery.

Self-Doubt: The Quiet Opponent

Alongside fatigue comes its quieter companion, doubt. You start questioning your worth, your direction, even your purpose.

Psychologists refer to this as the impostor phenomenon, the persistent fear of being exposed as inadequate despite evidence of success (Clance & Imes, 1978). Research suggests it affects high-achieving individuals across all fields, often during periods of transition or rapid growth (Vergauwe et al., 2015).

For me, doubt surfaced not at the start of my career, but after I had achieved stability. The external markers of success, such as titles and recognition, were there, but internally, I wondered if I was still growing or just maintaining.

What I've learned since is that doubt is not the enemy. It's a mirror. It shows where we've outgrown old definitions of ourselves. It invites reflection, not retreat.

When you stop fearing doubt and start listening to it, you discover where realignment is needed.

Realignment: Rediscovering Purpose

Realignment is the art of adjusting form without abandoning the race. It's not quitting; it's recalibrating.

Athletes make micro-adjustments mid-race, tweaking posture, stride, or breathing to maintain efficiency. Life demands the same. Sometimes realignment means changing careers, setting boundaries, or redefining success.

Research on purpose and well-being shows that individuals with a clear sense of meaning experience lower burnout, stronger resilience, and longer lifespan (Hill & Turiano, 2014). Purpose acts as psychological fuel; it gives fatigue somewhere to rest.

My realignment began when I realized my work had shifted from impact to output. I started asking new questions: What difference does this make? Who benefits from this effort? That shift from self-driven success to service-driven significance reignited the energy I'd lost.

Realignment doesn't always require reinvention. Sometimes it's simply remembering why you started running in the first place.

Mind, Body, and Spirit: Integrated Recovery

Physical rest alone isn't enough. The body can stop moving while the mind keeps racing. Sustainable recovery requires integration, tending to physical, emotional, and spiritual dimensions.

Mindfulness practices, gratitude journaling, and reflective solitude have been shown to reduce burnout and increase emotional regulation (Shapiro et al., 2007). Exercise, nutrition, and consistent sleep patterns reinforce that balance.

But perhaps the most overlooked form of recovery is spiritual reconnecting with something larger than oneself. Whether through faith, nature, art, or community, meaning must be renewed regularly. Without it, even success becomes hollow.

When I began aligning the dimensions of body, mind, and purpose, the wind didn't stop blowing, but I grew stronger against it. I learned that peace doesn't come from escape but from alignment.

You can't outrun the wind. You can only learn to lean into it wisely.

Leadership and the Courage to Pause

In leadership, admitting fatigue feels risky. Many fear that acknowledging burnout undermines authority. But the opposite is true: vulnerability strengthens trust.

Research on authentic leadership finds that transparency and emotional honesty improve employee engagement and organizational trust (Avolio & Gardner, 2005). When leaders model rest and self-awareness, teams follow suit.

I once had a team member approach me after a particularly intense project. "I thought you never got tired," she said. That comment startled me. It meant I'd modeled perfection, not humanity. From that point forward, I made a commitment to lead openly: to talk about limits, to normalize self-care, to encourage breaks.

Strong leaders don't shield others from reality; they teach them how to run sustainably through it.

Personal Reflections

I can still remember standing on the track on a windy afternoon, watching my athletes struggle against the gusts. Some leaned forward too much and lost balance; others tensed up and slowed. I told them, "The wind isn't the enemy, it's your resistance coach."

That lesson came back years later in my own life. The "wind" became the weight of deadlines, expectations, and fatigue. I tried to overpower it instead of adapting to it. Eventually, it taught me humility.

When I finally paused long enough to breathe, I rediscovered stillness. I started journaling again, reconnecting with mentors, and saying no more often. I realized that running through the wind had made me strong, but slowing down in it made me wise.

Now, when I feel that pressure return, I remind myself: lean, don't resist. Let the wind refine your form. It's not there to stop you, it's there to strengthen your stride.

Conclusion

The weight of the wind is unavoidable. Every runner, every leader, every person eventually faces resistance. Burnout and doubt are not signs of failure; they are invitations to recalibrate.

Life will test your endurance, but endurance is more than stamina; it's strategy. When fatigue arrives, don't quit. Realign. Rest. Rediscover your reason for running.

Because after the backstretch comes the curve, and those who've learned to breathe in the wind will handle that bend with grace.

References

Avolio, B. J., & Gardner, W. L. (2005). Authentic leadership development: Getting to the root of positive forms of leadership. The Leadership Quarterly, 16(3), 315–338.

Clance, P. R., & Imes, S. A. (1978). The impostor phenomenon in high achieving women: Dynamics and therapeutic intervention. Psychotherapy: Theory, Research & Practice, 15(3), 241–247.

Hill, P. L., & Turiano, N. A. (2014). Purpose in life as a predictor of mortality across adulthood. Psychological Science, 25(7), 1482–1486.

Kuhnel, J., Sonnentag, S., & Bledow, R. (2017). Resources and time pressure as day-level antecedents of work engagement. Journal of Occupational and Organizational Psychology, 90(2), 135–157.

Leiter, M. P., & Maslach, C. (2009). Nurse turnover: The mediating role of burnout. Journal of Nursing Management, 17(3), 331–339.

Maslach, C. (2003). Burnout: The cost of caring. Malor Books.

Shapiro, S. L., Astin, J. A., Bishop, S. R., & Cordova, M. (2007). Mindfulness-based stress reduction for health care professionals: Results from a randomized trial. International Journal of Stress Management, 12(2), 164–176.

Vergauwe, J., Wille, B., Feys, M., De Fruyt, F., & Anseel, F. (2015). Fear of being exposed: The trait-relatedness of the impostor phenomenon and its relevance in the work context. Journal of Business and Psychology, 30(3), 565–581.

Walker, M. (2017). Why we sleep: Unlocking the power of sleep and dreams. Scribner.

World Health Organization. (2019). Burn-out an "occupational phenomenon": International Classification of Diseases.

Part III

The Curve (41–60 Years):

Reflection and Adjustment

Chapter 7

The Bend of Time

Wisdom and Reinvention

Key Learnings:

- Midlife is not a decline; it's a pivot point for rediscovery and reinvention.
- Experience becomes the new form of strength when raw energy fades.
- Emotional flexibility and humility sustain relevance through change.
- Reinvention requires unlearning, not just learning.
- Wisdom emerges when ambition and perspective finally find balance.

Introduction: Entering the Curve

In a 400-meter race, the curve is where things get real. You've burned through much of your energy, and the body begins to argue with the mind. This is where runners must trust their training. The curve feels endless, but those who've paced themselves know that how you handle it determines how you finish.

In life, the curve represents the 40s and 50s, a period when many begin to feel the weight of time. Careers plateau, children grow up, parents age, and the mirror becomes more honest. The world seems to move faster, and you realize you can't simply sprint through it anymore. You have to run smarter.

Yet, for all its challenges, the curve is also the most revealing. It's where vision sharpens, priorities crystallize, and reinvention begins. The first half of the race was about proving yourself. The curve is about becoming yourself.

The Myth of the Midlife Crisis

The term "midlife crisis" was coined by psychologist Elliott Jaques in 1965, but modern research challenges its universality. While some experience turbulence in midlife, many find it to be a time of growth, clarity, and renewed purpose (Lachman, 2015).

Instead of a crisis, think of it as a correction. You start assessing what matters. You question whether your path still aligns with your purpose. Erik Erikson (1950) described this as the stage of generativity vs. stagnation, characterized by the desire to contribute meaningfully to others rather than to chase personal validation.

In my own journey, midlife didn't hit as panic; it arrived as a reflection. I began asking quieter but more powerful questions: Is my work still meaningful? Am I growing or just repeating patterns? What legacy am I building?

These questions weren't signs of crisis; they were signs of consciousness. They forced me to slow down, examine the map, and adjust direction before the final stretch.

Reinvention: The Art of Unlearning

Reinvention isn't always about doing something new, it's about doing the old things with new awareness.

In a world that glorifies constant innovation, we often overlook the wisdom of unlearning, letting go of beliefs, habits, and fears that no longer serve us. Research on adult learning theory suggests that midlife learners thrive when they reframe challenges as opportunities for mastery rather than threats to identity (Mezirow, 2000).

When I transitioned into new leadership roles, I had to unlearn the need for control. I'd built success by being hands-on, but growth demanded trust. Reinvention required less doing, more guiding. That unlearning opened space for others to rise and for me to evolve.

Unlearning also applies personally. It's about letting go of rigid definitions of success, beauty, and worth. The body changes, priorities shift, and what once mattered begins to fade. But in that shedding, a truer self begins to emerge.

As Carl Jung wrote, "We cannot live the afternoon of life according to the program of life's morning." The curve requires a new stride.

Wisdom as a Form of Strength

At this stage, physical stamina may wane, but cognitive and emotional endurance peak. Neuroscience shows that emotional regulation, pattern recognition, and decision-making improve with age (Carstensen et al., 2011).

Wisdom, in many ways, is the reward of surviving the earlier laps. You've been knocked down enough to know what matters. You've learned the cost of ego and the value of empathy.

In leadership, wisdom looks like restraint, the pause before reacting, the space before judging. It's understanding that every problem doesn't need solving; some just need understanding.

Wisdom also shows up in humility. You begin to realize that being right is less important than being kind, and that control is often an illusion. The runner who grips too tightly loses form. The wise runner learns to flow.

Relationships and the Changing Pace of Connection

As the curve of life bends, relationships evolve. Children leave home, friendships mature, and marriages either deepen or drift.

Research by socioemotional selectivity theorist Laura Carstensen (2011) found that as people age, they prioritize emotionally meaningful relationships over superficial ones. The social circle narrows, but depth increases.

In my own life, I noticed that my circle became smaller but stronger. Conversations grew more honest. I stopped pretending to be fine when I wasn't. There's liberation in authenticity, as it attracts people who value truth over performance.

This stage invites reconciliation, making peace with family, forgiving past mistakes, and cherishing time with those who remain. Relationships become less about shared activity and more about shared meaning.

The Mirror and the Mind: Aging with Purpose

The curve also brings physical and existential awareness. You begin to see changes; gray hair, slower recovery, maybe a few aches that didn't exist before. But aging, as Harvard researcher George Vaillant (2002) observed, can bring increased resilience and emotional depth when one lives with purpose and gratitude.

Aging gracefully doesn't mean surrendering to decline; it means embracing evolution. Every wrinkle is a footnote of survival. Every scar is a reminder that life was lived fully.

For me, the mirror stopped being an enemy when I stopped expecting it to reflect who I was and started appreciating who I'd become. The goal isn't to outrun time, it's to move with it, learning to let each day teach you something new.

Faith, Meaning, and Legacy

At this stage, many rediscover faith not necessarily in religion, but in purpose. Faith is what gives suffering meaning and turns aging into awakening.

Research on existential well-being shows that people with a strong sense of purpose or spirituality report higher life satisfaction and lower depression in midlife (Schnell, 2009). Faith, however one defines it, anchors the spirit through uncertainty.

Legacy also takes center stage. Legacy isn't just what you leave behind; it's what you build while you're still here. It's mentoring the next generation, creating something lasting, or simply living with integrity so your example becomes your echo.

As I grew older, I began to care less about being remembered for achievements and more about being remembered for impact. Titles fade, but influence endures.

Personal Reflections

I think of the curve often when I look back on my life. There was a time when I believed the curve was where you slowed down, where you started losing ground. But I've learned it's actually where you find your form.

When I hit my own "curve years," I began reevaluating everything: career, health, faith, and relationships. I didn't panic; I listened. I realized I no longer needed to prove I could run fast. I needed to run true.

I began spending more time mentoring others, writing, traveling, and reflecting. Reinvention didn't mean starting over; it meant starting deeper.

There's peace in accepting that the curve is not punishment, it's perspective. It teaches that wisdom isn't about speed, it's about stride. I don't run like I did at 25, but my rhythm now carries something 25 never had: grace.

Conclusion

The curve of life is where strength transforms into wisdom, and ambition matures into purpose. It's not the beginning of decline; it's the beginning of depth.

If the early race was about proving capability, the curve is about proving character. It's where resilience becomes rhythm and experience becomes your guide.

Handle the bend with courage, and you'll find that the home stretch ahead is something to savor, not something to fear.

References

Carstensen, L. L., Fung, H. H., & Charles, S. T. (2011). Socioemotional selectivity theory and the regulation of emotion in adulthood. Motivation and Emotion, 25(2), 103–123.

Erikson, E. H. (1950). Childhood and society. W. W. Norton & Company.

Jaques, E. (1965). Death and the midlife crisis. International Journal of Psychoanalysis, 46, 502–514.

Lachman, M. E. (2015). Mind the gap in the middle: A call to study midlife. Research in Human Development, 12(3-4), 327–334.

Mezirow, J. (2000). Learning as transformation: Critical perspectives on a theory in progress. Jossey-Bass.

Schnell, T. (2009). The sources of meaning and meaning in life questionnaire (SoMe): Relations to demographics and well-being. The Journal of Positive Psychology, 4(6), 483–499.

Vaillant, G. E. (2002). Aging well: Surprising guideposts to a happier life from the landmark Harvard study of adult development. Little, Brown and Company.

Chapter 8

The Fastest 100

Purpose, Legacy, and Fulfillment

Key Learnings:

- The "fastest 100" is not about physical speed it's about clarity and alignment.
- Purpose-driven living creates momentum that outlasts ambition.
- Legacy is built through consistent impact, not grand gestures.
- Gratitude, mentorship, and authenticity amplify meaning in this stage of life.
- True fulfillment comes from contribution, not accumulation.

Introduction: When the Stride Feels Effortless

In the 400-meter race, the stretch after the curve can feel exhilarating. Once runners exit the bend, they catch a glimpse of the finish line. The form is set, the rhythm is established, and adrenaline kicks in. It's often the fastest part of the race, not because the body is fresher, but because the mind is fully engaged.

Life works the same way. The years between your mid-40s and early 60s can be among the most productive, purposeful, and powerful. You've learned to manage energy instead of chasing it, to work with your limits instead of against them. Experience becomes a multiplier. The vision ahead sharpens, and the question shifts from What can I get? to What can I give?

This is the fastest 100 is not of youth, but of legacy. It's when life starts to reveal what all the earlier effort was for.

Purpose: The Fuel for the Second Wind

Purpose is the strongest performance enhancer known to humanity. Studies show that individuals with a clear sense of purpose experience better physical health, a lower risk of cognitive decline, and a longer lifespan (Ryff & Singer, 2008). Purpose aligns behavior with meaning, giving energy a destination.

In this stage, purpose is less about self-advancement and more about contribution. Many people find new direction through mentoring, teaching, volunteering, or building something that will outlast them.

I learned this firsthand. In my earlier years, I ran on drive; in midlife, I began running on meaning. When I started mentoring younger professionals, I realized that leadership was never about control; it was about cultivation. Watching others grow became more fulfilling than any personal milestone.

Purpose, at its core, is service. It transforms effort into impact and turns ordinary work into legacy.

Legacy: The Echo You Leave Behind

Legacy isn't written in obituaries; it's felt in influence. It's what people remember because of how you made them feel, what you taught them, and how you showed up.

Sociologist Dan McAdams (2001) described legacy through the concept of generativity or the drive to guide the next generation. Research suggests that individuals who invest in generativity report higher life satisfaction and emotional well-being, particularly in midlife (Grossbaum & Bates, 2002).

For me, legacy became less about "leaving something behind" and more about "building something lasting." I realized that my influence wasn't just in what I did, but in who I helped others become. The quiet moments of listening, advising, and supporting became the race's most meaningful strides.

Legacy is not the victory lap; it's the track you leave for others to run.

Fulfillment vs. Success

By this stage, many realize that success and fulfillment aren't synonyms. Success is external titles, status, and accomplishments. Fulfillment is internal peace, gratitude, and alignment.

Research in positive psychology highlights that fulfillment derives from autonomy, mastery, and purpose rather than wealth or recognition (Seligman, 2011). People at midlife who pivot toward work and relationships that align with intrinsic values report greater overall happiness (King & Hicks, 2009).

In my earlier years, I defined success by motion: more projects, more progress. Now, I measure it by the meaning depth of impact, authenticity, and balance. I've learned that fulfillment doesn't come from finishing the race faster; it comes from running it well.

This stage invites us to rewrite our definitions: success fades, but fulfillment endures.

Gratitude as Acceleration

Gratitude is the secret energy of the fastest 100. It turns memory into momentum. Studies consistently link gratitude to higher emotional resilience, better health, and stronger relationships (Emmons & McCullough, 2003). Gratitude doesn't erase hardship, it reframes it as evidence of endurance.

In my life, gratitude became a practice, not a mood. I began ending each day by reflecting on three things that went right, no matter how small. That habit shifted my attention from what was missing to what was meaningful.

Gratitude doesn't just make you feel better, it makes you run better. It lightens the load of regret and focuses energy on what's still possible.

Mentorship and Multiplication

At this point, your wisdom is your greatest asset, and sharing it multiplies its value. Mentorship turns individual experience into collective progress.

A 2019 study by Allen and Eby found that mentors experience higher job satisfaction and psychological well-being than non-mentors. Teaching reinforces learning; guiding others strengthens self-awareness.

When I mentor, I'm reminded of my younger self the uncertainty, the hunger, the fear of falling behind. I tell them what I wish I'd heard: It's okay to slow down, as long as you stay intentional. Mentorship, I've realized, is how we pass the baton not by giving away our race, but by helping others find theirs.

Authenticity: The Freedom of the Fastest 100

The fastest strides of life are also the most authentic ones. You've lived enough to know what matters and survived enough to stop pretending.

Authenticity, the alignment between values and actions, is strongly correlated with psychological well-being (Wood et al., 2008). It allows you to show up as your whole self without fear of judgment.

For me, authenticity came when I stopped editing my story to fit expectations. I began writing, speaking, and leading from experience, not performance. The irony is that the more real you become, the faster your influence grows because truth travels farther than image.

The fastest 100 is where you run unmasked.

Personal Reflections

When I think about this stretch of life, I picture a runner emerging from the curve and seeing the straightaway ahead. The lungs burn, the legs ache, but the heart feels alive. This is where all the training pays off, where wisdom and endurance finally sync.

For me, this stage has been less about reaching milestones and more about creating meaning. I've watched the people I've mentored thrive, the ideas I've planted take root, and the lessons I've learned in struggle turn into stories that help others.

I no longer run to prove I can; I run because I love the race. There's freedom in that freedom in knowing that the finish line isn't the goal. The goal is to run the last stretch with gratitude, generosity, and grace.

Conclusion

The fastest 100 of life isn't powered by youth, it's powered by purpose. It's when clarity overtakes confusion, gratitude outruns greed, and meaning becomes momentum.

Those who embrace this stage discover that fulfillment doesn't come from adding more but from deepening what already is. Purpose sharpens vision. Gratitude strengthens stride. Legacy ensures that the race continues long after your own finish.

When your life begins to accelerate again, don't resist it. Just keep your eyes forward, your form steady, and your heart open. Because this is what all the running was for.

References

Allen, T. D., & Eby, L. T. (2019). The Blackwell handbook of mentoring: A multiple perspectives approach. Wiley-Blackwell.

Emmons, R. A., & McCullough, M. E. (2003). Counting blessings versus burdens: An experimental investigation of gratitude and subjective well-being in daily life. Journal of Personality and Social Psychology, 84(2), 377–389.

Grossbaum, M. F., & Bates, G. W. (2002). Correlates of generativity in adulthood: Age, gender, education, and family status. Journal of Adult Development, 9(2), 87–99.

King, L. A., & Hicks, J. A. (2009). Detecting and constructing meaning in life events. The Journal of Positive Psychology, 4(5), 317–330.

McAdams, D. P. (2001). The psychology of life stories. Review of General Psychology, 5(2), 100–122.

Ryff, C. D., & Singer, B. (2008). Know thyself and become what you are: A eudaimonic approach to psychological well-being. Journal of Happiness Studies, 9(1), 13–39.

Seligman, M. E. P. (2011). Flourish: A visionary new understanding of happiness and well-being. Free Press.

Wood, A. M., Linley, P. A., Maltby, J., Baliousis, M., & Joseph, S. (2008). The authentic personality: A theoretical and empirical conceptualization and the development of the Authenticity Scale. Journal of Counseling Psychology, 55(3), 385–399.

Chapter 9

The Unexpected Stumble

Resilience, Renewal, and Grace

Key Learnings:

- Setbacks are inevitable; resilience is learned through recovery, not resistance.
- Renewal begins when you accept that failure is feedback, not finality.
- Grace under pressure transforms hardship into wisdom.
- Vulnerability and support systems are the foundation of lasting resilience.
- The stumble refines character more deeply than success ever can.

Introduction: The Moment You Fall

In the 400-meter race, there's nothing more jarring than tripping mid-stride. The body moves faster than the mind, and in an instant, you're on the ground. Every runner knows that moment of the gasp, the shock, the disbelief. But what separates good runners from great ones isn't that they never fall; it's that they get up fast, regain form, and finish with dignity.

Life works the same way. The stumble could be a career setback, a health diagnosis, a broken relationship, or a loss that changes everything. It's the moment the plan collapses and the wind is knocked out of you. The first instinct is to ask, Why me? But over time, that question becomes, What now?

The stumble reveals truth: that resilience isn't about toughness, it's about trust. Trust in yourself, in your process, and in life's ability to rebuild what's been shaken.

The Anatomy of Resilience

Resilience is not an innate trait; it's a practiced skill. Psychologist Ann Masten (2001) called it "ordinary magic," emphasizing that resilience is built through everyday habits, not heroic acts. It's the ability to adapt successfully in the face of adversity.

Research shows that resilient individuals share three characteristics: connection, competence, and confidence (Southwick & Charney, 2012). They rely on relationships, build problem-solving skills, and maintain faith in their ability to influence outcomes.

During one difficult chapter of my life, I faced a personal and professional setback that tested every part of me. I felt disoriented, like my internal compass had broken. But resilience came in quiet forms: a supportive conversation, a walk, a prayer. Recovery didn't happen overnight; it happened one choice at a time.

The lesson: resilience doesn't roar. It whispers, Get up.

Failure as a Teacher

Failure carries its own form of education. Studies on post-traumatic growth show that individuals often report greater appreciation for life, deeper relationships, and stronger spiritual awareness after adversity (Tedeschi & Calhoun, 2004). Pain, paradoxically, can become a portal to wisdom.

For me, failure stripped away the illusion of control. It taught humility. It forced me to evaluate not just what I was doing, but why. When I finally understood that falling didn't mean I'd lost the race, only that I needed to adjust my stride, I started to heal.

The stumble teaches two things: the fragility of plans and the durability of spirit.

The Power of Vulnerability

After a fall, pride often prevents us from asking for help. But vulnerability is not weakness; it's strength in motion. Brené Brown (2012) defines vulnerability as the courage to be seen when you can't control the outcome.

Research supports that social support is the single greatest predictor of resilience and recovery (Ozbay et al., 2007). When we isolate, pain multiplies; when we connect, healing accelerates.

I've learned that sharing your story, especially in times of struggle, gives others permission to do the same. There's healing in honesty, and connection in transparency.

It takes courage to admit that you're not okay. But it's in that admission that grace enters.

Grace: The Art of Rising Well

Grace is resilience without resistance. It's the ability to get up without bitterness, to move forward without denial, and to forgive what broke you.

Psychologists define self-compassion as a close cousin of grace, as treating oneself with the same kindness offered to others. Research by Kristin Neff (2003) shows that self-compassion reduces depression and anxiety while increasing motivation.

I once believed that grace was passive acceptance. Now I understand it's active strength. It's not pretending the pain didn't happen it's choosing not to let it define you. Grace doesn't erase the scar; it dignifies it.

When we rise with grace, we not only heal we inspire.

Renewal: Turning Pain into Purpose

Every stumble carries the seed of renewal. The Japanese art of kintsugi repairs broken pottery with gold, highlighting cracks instead of hiding them. That's what renewal does: it turns the damage into design.

Research in narrative psychology shows that reframing painful experiences into coherent personal stories increases psychological well-being (Pennebaker & Seagal, 1999). Storytelling transforms suffering into structure; it gives meaning to the mess.

When I stumbled, I eventually turned the experience into a story. I began speaking openly about it, not to relive it, but to release it. That story became a bridge for others facing their own setbacks. Renewal, I discovered, is how resilience becomes service.

You rise not to erase what happened, but to help others rise too.

Faith, Forgiveness, and Forward Motion

Resilience and renewal are incomplete without forgiveness, both of others and yourself. Holding on to regret or resentment keeps you tied to the past.

Spiritual research consistently links forgiveness to emotional healing and reduced stress (Toussaint et al., 2001). It doesn't mean forgetting; it means freeing your energy to move forward.

Faith, whether in God, humanity, or simply the process of healing, restores direction when logic fails. During one of my lowest moments, I stopped trying to fix everything and simply said, "Show me the next step." That surrender didn't make me weaker; it made me lighter.

The stumble is never the end, it's the threshold of something wiser.

Personal Reflections

There was a season when I fell hard. Not physically, but emotionally and professionally. The plan unraveled, and for a while, so did I. I kept replaying everything, looking for the mistake, trying to rewind the moment before the stumble.

But life doesn't let you rewind, it invites you to rebuild.

What saved me wasn't strength; it was softness. The willingness to rest, to listen, to lean on others. I learned that courage isn't running without fear; it's running through fear with faith.

When I finally got back up, I didn't try to sprint. I walked first. I rebuilt my rhythm slowly. I learned to trust the ground again. And when I began running once more, I ran differently, not to win, but to finish well.

That's the grace of the stumble, it changes how you move forever.

Conclusion

The unexpected stumble is the most honest part of the race. It strips away ego and reveals endurance. It teaches that strength isn't about avoiding falls but rising differently each time.

Resilience rebuilds. Renewal redefines. Grace redeems.

When you stumble and you will remember this: the race doesn't end with the fall. Sometimes, that's where it truly begins.

References

Brown, B. (2012). Daring greatly: How the courage to be vulnerable transforms the way we live, love, parent, and lead. Gotham Books.

Masten, A. S. (2001). Ordinary magic: Resilience processes in development. American Psychologist, 56(3), 227–238.

Neff, K. D. (2003). Self-compassion: An alternative conceptualization of a healthy attitude toward oneself. Self and Identity, 2(2), 85–101.

Ozbay, F., Johnson, D. C., Dimoulas, E., Morgan, C. A., Charney, D., & Southwick, S. (2007). Social support and resilience to stress. Psychiatry, 4(5), 35–40.

Pennebaker, J. W., & Seagal, J. D. (1999). Forming a story: The health benefits of narrative. Journal of Clinical Psychology, 55(10), 1243–1254.

Southwick, S. M., & Charney, D. S. (2012). Resilience: The science of mastering life's greatest challenges. Cambridge University Press.

Tedeschi, R. G., & Calhoun, L. G. (2004). Posttraumatic growth: Conceptual foundations and empirical evidence. Psychological Inquiry, 15(1), 1–18.

Toussaint, L., Williams, D. R., Musick, M. A., & Everson, S. A. (2001). Forgiveness and health: Age differences in a U.S. probability sample. Journal of Adult Development, 8(4), 249–257.

Part IV

The Home Stretch (Ages 61–80+)

Grace and Fulfillment

Chapter 10

The Homestretch

Wisdom, Reflection, and Peace

Key Learnings:

- The home stretch of life is less about speed and more about savoring the journey.
- Peace comes not from perfection, but from acceptance and gratitude.
- Reflection transforms memory into wisdom and regret into growth.
- Community, legacy, and purpose remain the pillars of lasting fulfillment.
- The finish line is not an ending it's a transition into meaning.

Introduction: The Finish Line in Sight

Every 400-meter runner knows the home stretch well. The lungs burn, the legs tremble, but the finish line finally appears. For some, it's a signal of exhaustion; for others, it's liberation. The last 100 meters aren't just about strength, they're about resolve, rhythm, and grace.

Life's final stretch feels much the same. These are the years when the noise quiets and clarity takes the lead. The frantic striving of youth gives way to peace, the obsession with progress to gratitude. You see the patterns, the people, and the purpose more clearly now. The wisdom once buried under ambition rises to the surface.

This stage isn't about how much distance is left, it's about how beautifully you finish.

The Psychology of Reflection

Reflection is more than reminiscing; it's the brain's way of finding meaning. Psychologist Erik Erikson (1950) described late adulthood as the stage of integrity vs. despair. Integrity comes when people can look back on their triumphs and mistakes with peace. Despair arises when regrets overshadow gratitude.

Research confirms that reflective thinking in older adulthood improves emotional regulation and reduces depression (Jeste & Oswald, 2014). Reflection allows the mind to integrate life's experiences into a coherent story, a personal narrative that affirms value and purpose.

In my own reflections, I've found that the most meaningful moments weren't the loud ones. They were the quiet mornings, the simple victories, the relationships that outlasted time. Reflection gives shape to life. It's the moment you realize that even the painful chapters were necessary to complete the story.

The Gift of Perspective

One of the greatest rewards of age is perspective. The things that once felt catastrophic now seem instructive. The storms that once felt endless now appear as brief seasons of growth.

Neuroscience supports this. As people age, emotional responses to stress tend to soften, and empathy increases (Carstensen et al., 2011). Perspective is the emotional distance earned through years of living, an ability to see events not as failures but as feedback.

I've learned to say "It was worth it" about things I once wished away. Every risk, every heartbreak, every late night they all led here. Perspective doesn't erase pain; it redeems it.

Peace as the Final Rhythm

Peace is not the absence of noise, it's harmony with it.

Philosophers from Marcus Aurelius to Thich Nhat Hanh have described peace as acceptance of impermanence. Psychologists echo this idea: inner peace stems from aligning expectations with reality (Fleeson & Jayawickreme, 2015).

In these later years, peace comes from simplification. You realize you don't need as much. One looks for less noise, fewer possessions, smaller circles, and deeper meaning. Time becomes the true luxury.

I used to chase more; now I value enough. Enough love, enough laughter, enough light in each day to remind me I'm still part of something beautiful.

Peace is not something you find at the end; it's something you practice at every step along the way.

Legacy and Continuity

As the body slows, the spirit seeks continuity. Legacy becomes less about name and more about nurture. It's knowing that your actions, however small, ripple beyond your lifetime.

Psychological studies on symbolic immortality (Lifton, 1974) suggest that leaving meaningful contributions behind, such as children, mentorship, and community involvement, provides comfort in later life. It assures us that our story continues even when we no longer write it.

For me, legacy now looks like the lives I've touched, the people I've mentored, the words I've written. Every kind act, every story shared, every lesson passed forward, they are the footprints that remain after the race.

We spend so much of life building resumes; in the home stretch, we build relationships that outlive them.

Gratitude and Letting Go

The home stretch teaches one of life's hardest lessons: letting go with grace. Children grow, friends pass, the body slows, the world moves on. Yet, gratitude transforms loss into legacy.

Studies show that gratitude in later life is linked to improved sleep, reduced stress, and greater satisfaction (Krause, 2006). Gratitude is the psychological bridge between what was and what remains.

I've found that gratitude allows space for both joy and grief. I can miss the past while still loving the present. Letting go doesn't mean forgetting; it means freeing both yourself and those you love to continue their own races.

Community and Connection

Loneliness is one of the great challenges of aging, but community restores meaning. The Harvard Study of Adult Development, which tracked participants for over 80 years, concluded that close relationships, not wealth or fame, predict lifelong happiness (Waldinger & Schulz, 2010).

The home stretch reminds us that we were never meant to run alone. Whether through family, faith, or friendship, connection keeps the spirit alive.

For me, this has meant spending more time in presence than in productivity. Listening more. Laughing more. Sitting quietly with people I love without needing to say anything profound.

Connection, in the end, is the finish line we were always running toward.

Personal Reflections

I often think about how my stride has changed. The power I once found in speed, I now find in stillness. The need to prove has faded, replaced by a desire to give.

There's a certain beauty in reaching this stretch of life. You begin to realize that peace isn't earned, it's allowed. You start giving yourself permission to rest, to forgive, to be grateful for simply being here.

I walk more than I run now, but my pace is filled with purpose. I spend time with people I love, tell stories that matter, and take joy in the smallest things like sunrise, laughter, or a shared meal.

The home stretch has taught me that finishing well doesn't mean finishing first. It means crossing the line with grace, gratitude, and love in your heart.

Conclusion

The home stretch is not the end of the race; it's the fulfillment of it. It's where wisdom ripens, reflection deepens, and peace takes its rightful place as the measure of success.

When you reach this stage, don't look back with regret or forward with fear. Look inward with appreciation. You've earned the right to rest, to reflect, and to rejoice in the simple truth that you ran the race fully.

Because in the end, it's not about how fast you ran, it's about how fully you lived.

References

Carstensen, L. L., Fung, H. H., & Charles, S. T. (2011). Socioemotional selectivity theory and the regulation of emotion in adulthood. Motivation and Emotion, 25(2), 103–123.

Erikson, E. H. (1950). Childhood and society. W. W. Norton & Company.

Fleeson, W., & Jayawickreme, E. (2015). Whole trait theory. Journal of Research in Personality, 56, 82–92.

Jeste, D. V., & Oswald, A. J. (2014). Wisdom and well-being in aging. Annual Review of Gerontology and Geriatrics, 34(1), 1–21.

Krause, N. (2006). Gratitude toward God, stress, and health in late life. Research on Aging, 28(2), 163–183.

Lifton, R. J. (1974). The broken connection: On death and the continuity of life. Simon & Schuster.

Waldinger, R. J., & Schulz, M. S. (2010). What makes a good life? Lessons from the Harvard Study of Adult Development. Harvard Gazette.

Chapter 11

Fighting Fatigue

Staying Strong Until the End

Key Learnings:

- Longevity is not just about years added, but quality sustained.
- Mental resilience, physical care, and social connection preserve strength in later life.
- Purpose and movement, both literal and metaphorical, keep the spirit alive.
- Acceptance and adaptability are the true measures of vitality.
- Aging gracefully means continuing the race with faith, humor, and self-compassion.

Introduction: When the Legs Grow Heavy

In the 400-meter race, the final 50 meters are pure will. The lactic acid burns, the lungs tighten, and the legs feel like lead. Every instinct says slow down, but the great runners push through, not because they have more energy, but because they have more heart.

Life's final stretch feels the same. Physical, emotional, and existential fatigue set in. The body speaks louder than the mind. But for those who've cultivated purpose, faith, and gratitude, there's still rhythm in the stride. You learn to move not through force, but through flow.

This chapter is not about defying age. It's about dancing with it. Staying strong until the end isn't about resistance; it's about relationships. With your body, your time, and your truth.

The Science of Aging Well

Aging well is an art grounded in science. Research from Harvard's Adult Development Study (Vaillant, 2002) found that happiness in late life correlates strongly with emotional stability, physical health, and close relationships, not wealth or fame.

Physical activity remains a critical factor. Regular moderate exercise lowers risk for heart disease, cognitive decline, and depression (Nelson et al., 2007). Equally important is maintaining cognitive elasticity, keeping the brain challenged through reading, puzzles, or learning new skills (Park et al., 2014).

But the research also reveals something deeper: attitude predicts aging outcomes as much as lifestyle. People who view aging positively live, on average, seven years longer than those who see it as decline (Levy et al., 2002).

The body follows the story the mind believes. If you define aging as ending, the spirit slows first.

The Mind-Body Connection

The home stretch demands awareness of the profound dialogue between body and mind. What we think, we feel; what we feel, we become.

Psychoneuroimmunology research (Ader & Cohen, 1993) shows that mindset directly affects immune and inflammatory responses. Optimism, humor, and gratitude reduce physiological stress markers and strengthen resilience.

I've noticed this truth in others and myself: when people stop moving mentally or physically, decline accelerates. But when they remain curious about ideas, people, or even their own inner world, they stay vibrant.

Movement, I've learned, is medicine. It doesn't have to be running; it can be walking, gardening, dancing, or writing. Every act of engagement says to life, I'm still here.

Purpose as Energy

Purpose doesn't retire when the job does. In fact, it becomes even more essential.

Research by Patricia Boyle and colleagues (2010) found that having a sense of purpose in older adulthood significantly reduces the risk of cognitive decline and mortality. Purpose acts like a psychological battery; it keeps the heart and mind charged.

For many, purpose in later years emerges through mentoring, volunteering, creative pursuits, or simply being present for family. It doesn't have to be grand; it just has to be yours.

When I began writing and teaching in my later career, I found my second wind. I realized purpose doesn't diminish with age, it deepens. The urgency fades, replaced by clarity. What once felt like effort now feels like offering.

Accepting the Body's Conversation

The body, once a vessel of ambition, becomes a teacher of humility. Joints stiffen, sleep changes, healing slows. But these signals are communication, not punishment.

Gerontologists describe selective optimization with compensation (Baltes & Baltes, 1990) as the process by which older adults adapt to limitations by focusing on strengths and adjusting strategies. Runners call it "listening to the legs."

For me, this meant letting go of perfection. Instead of chasing the pace I once had, I learned to celebrate consistency. Some days, strength looks like a full workout; other days, it's a mindful walk. The key is presence, not performance.

Acceptance doesn't mean surrender; it means stewardship. The body changes, but the will to move remains sacred.

Faith, Humor, and Perspective

Endurance in later life depends as much on spirit as on structure. Faith and humor are twin anchors of resilience.

Faith provides meaning when logic falters. It reframes mortality not as an end, but as a homecoming. Studies show that spiritual engagement increases life satisfaction and reduces anxiety about aging (Koenig, 2012).

Humor, meanwhile, is the emotional oxygen of aging. Laughing at the body's quirks and life's ironies transforms frustration into grace.

Viktor Frankl (1959) called humor "another of the soul's weapons in the fight for self-preservation."

I've learned to laugh at the stiffness, to thank the mirror for honesty, and to see each day as a gift, not a guarantee. Humor keeps the spirit light enough to keep running.

The Art of Slowing Without Stopping

There comes a time when slowing down is not a choice but a calling. The trick is to do it with intention.

In the later stages of the race, runners focus less on acceleration and more on form. They lift their chests, keep their eyes forward, and finish strong. In life, slowing means savoring. It's turning from quantity to quality, from doing more to being more.

Research shows that mindfulness practices in older adults reduce pain perception, improve focus, and enhance life satisfaction (Geiger et al., 2016). Presence becomes the new performance.

I used to think rest was something earned after the work was done. Now I know the rest is the work. It's the discipline of peace.

Personal Reflections

I used to fear slowing down. I thought it meant losing relevance. But as the years unfolded, I discovered the opposite: slowing down brought me closer to what mattered.

I wake up earlier now, not to work, but to watch the sunrise. I take longer walks, not to burn calories, but to remember gratitude. My conversations are fewer but richer, and my days are quieter but fuller.

There are moments when fatigue whispers, but I've learned to listen not to stop, but to pace. The finish line doesn't frighten me anymore. It reminds me to keep running with grace, purpose, and love.

Strength isn't how long you can run; it's how fully you can live when running becomes walking, and walking becomes presence.

Conclusion

Fighting fatigue isn't about denying time; it's about defining it. The strongest runners are those who respect both the body's limits and the soul's boundlessness.

In the final stretch, vitality is found not in resistance, but in rhythm. Keep moving, keep laughing, keep believing. Let every breath remind you that life, even near its end, is still a race worth running.

And when the finish line comes into view, meet it not with fear, but with gratitude. Because by then, you'll realize you didn't just run the race, you embodied it.

References

Ader, R., & Cohen, N. (1993). Psychoneuroimmunology: Conditioning and stress. Annual Review of Psychology, 44(1), 53–85.

Baltes, P. B., & Baltes, M. M. (1990). Successful aging: Perspectives from the behavioral sciences. Cambridge University Press.

Boyle, P. A., Barnes, L. L., Buchman, A. S., & Bennett, D. A. (2010). Purpose in life is associated with mortality among older adults. Psychosomatic Medicine, 72(7), 676–683.

Frankl, V. E. (1959). Man's search for meaning. Beacon Press.

Geiger, P. J., Boggero, I. A., Brake, C. A., Caldera, C. A., Combs, H. L., Peters, J. R., & Baer, R. A. (2016). Mindfulness-based interventions for older adults: A review of the effects on physical and emotional well-being. Mindfulness, 7(2), 296–307.

Koenig, H. G. (2012). Religion, spirituality, and health: The research and clinical implications. ISRN Psychiatry, 2012, 278730.

Levy, B. R., Slade, M. D., Kunkel, S. R., & Kasl, S. V. (2002). Longevity increased by positive self-perceptions of aging. Journal of Personality and Social Psychology, 83(2), 261–270.

Nelson, M. E., Rejeski, W. J., Blair, S. N., Duncan, P. W., Judge, J. O., King, A. C., ... & Castaneda-Sceppa, C. (2007). Physical activity and public health in older adults: Recommendation from the American College of Sports Medicine and the American Heart Association. Circulation, 116(9), 1094–1105.

Park, D. C., Lodi-Smith, J., Drew, L., Haber, S., Hebrank, A., Bischof, G. N., & Aamodt, W. (2014). The impact of sustained engagement on cognitive function in older adults. Psychological Science, 25(1), 103–112.

Vaillant, G. E. (2002). Aging well: Surprising guideposts to a happier life from the Harvard study of adult development. Little, Brown and Company.

Chapter 12

The Finish Line

Legacy and Light

Key Learnings:

- The finish line of life is not an end but a transformation of meaning and memory.
- Legacy is the echo of your choices, values, and love across time.
- Peace at the finish comes from acceptance, gratitude, and reconciliation.
- Death loses its power when life has been lived with purpose.
- Light, not fear, defines the final stride.

Introduction: The Line That Defines the Race

In the 400-meter race, the finish line is paradoxical; it marks both an end and an arrival. Runners collapse not from weakness, but from release. The body gives out just as the spirit soars. That last stride, as your chest crosses the line, is a surrender, letting go of everything you've carried.

In life, the finish line mirrors that same truth. It's not death itself that matters most; it's how we arrive there. With bitterness or grace? With regret or gratitude? With fear or with faith?

By the time you reach this stage, you've lived enough to know that time cannot be owned; it can only be honored. You begin to understand that legacy is not about leaving something behind, but about leaving something within others.

The race may end, but the light keeps traveling.

The Psychology of Completion

Humans have a deep need for closure, not to end the story, but to affirm that it mattered.

Research by psychologist Paul Wong (2010) on the meaning management theory suggests that people who face mortality with purpose, faith, and coherence experience higher levels of peace and life satisfaction. Facing the end with meaning transforms fear into acceptance.

Similarly, hospice pioneer Elisabeth Kübler-Ross (1969) observed that people who reconcile relationships, express gratitude, and forgive both themselves and others tend to die with remarkable serenity.

Completion, then, is about final understanding, not final words. It's realizing that life's race was never about perfection, but participation.

Legacy as Energy

Legacy isn't what you leave in a will, it's what you leave in the world. Sociologists call this generative transcendence the process by which your influence continues through others' actions, ideas, and memories (McAdams, 2001).

Legacy lives in the stories told at family gatherings, in the lessons passed on to students or children, and in the invisible ripple of kindness that shapes someone's day.

In my own reflection, I've realized that my legacy won't be measured in awards or titles, but in how I made people feel safer, wiser, or seen. The things I built may fade, but the impact of how I lived will echo far longer.

We are all both runners and relay givers. The baton we hand off is not work; it's wisdom.

The Spiritual Finish

Spirituality at life's end, religious or otherwise, often reframes mortality as transition, not termination. Research in thanatology (the study of death and dying) shows that people with a belief in continuity, whether it be the soul, legacy, or cosmic energy, report less fear and greater peace (Puchalski, 2012).

Faith provides language for mystery. It gives light to the unknown.

When I think about the finish line, I imagine it as crossing from shadow into sunlight. The body stops running, but the spirit keeps moving forward, carrying every lesson, every love, every ounce of gratitude.

Even if you don't believe in an afterlife, you can believe in after-love, the continuation of care, the ripple of goodness that outlives you.

Reconciliation and Release

The closer one gets to life's finish line, the more important forgiveness becomes. To carry resentment into the final stretch is like running with weights around your ankles.

Research by Worthington and Scherer (2004) found that forgiveness interventions in hospice settings reduce anxiety and increase life satisfaction. Releasing anger is not about excusing others; it's about freeing yourself from the emotional gravity of the past.

I've sat with people near their finish lines, friends, elders, mentors, and the peace they radiated wasn't born of denial. It was the serenity of having made peace with their story. They weren't trying to rewrite it anymore. They were simply reading the last page with gratitude.

To finish well, you must freely forgive yourself most of all.

The Body's Goodbye

As the race nears its end, the body begins its gentle surrender. The breath slows, the senses soften, and awareness turns inward. This stage, though often feared, is sacred in its simplicity.

Studies in palliative care show that many experience a surge of clarity, reconciliation, or even joy in their final days (Fenwick & Brayne, 2011). The human spirit, it seems, prepares itself for release.

In those moments, presence matters more than perfection. Whether surrounded by family, a quiet room, or even solitude, peace comes from knowing that nothing essential has been left unsaid.

The body may fade, but the light of the consciousness, the love, and the laughter shared remain imprinted in those we've touched.

Personal Reflections

I often imagine what that final stretch will feel like: the quiet, the slowing, the knowing. I don't fear it anymore. If anything, I hope I'll be aware enough to appreciate it to look back and whisper, That was a good race.

When my time comes, I don't want fanfare. I want laughter. I want the people I've loved to tell stories, not sorrows. I want them to know that I ran with all I had, stumbled plenty, but finished grateful.

I think about the baton I'll leave behind the ideas, the kindness, the lessons. I hope someone takes it and runs farther than I did. That's how races live on through continuation, not closure.

When I cross that finish line, I hope I still have breath left to say, Thank you. Because the privilege wasn't in finishing; it was in running.

Conclusion

The finish line of life is a bridge, not a boundary. It connects effort to eternity, body to spirit, and memory to legacy.

When your time comes, don't resist it. Reflect on the miles you've run, the people you've touched, and the lessons you've learned. Smile at the thought that even in stillness, your light keeps traveling forward.

Because in the end, the goal was never to outpace others, it was to illuminate the track for those still running.

And that light your light never fades.

References

Fenwick, P., & Brayne, S. (2011). End-of-life experiences: A guide for carers of the dying. American Journal of Hospice and Palliative Medicine, 28(1), 1–9.

Kübler-Ross, E. (1969). On death and dying. Macmillan.

McAdams, D. P. (2001). The psychology of life stories. Review of General Psychology, 5(2), 100–122.

Puchalski, C. M. (2012). Spirituality in health: The role of compassion in medicine. Southern Medical Journal, 105(12), 650–652.

Wong, P. T. P. (2010). Meaning therapy: An integrative and positive existential psychotherapy. Journal of Contemporary Psychotherapy, 40(2), 85–93.

Worthington, E. L., & Scherer, M. (2004). Forgiveness is an emotion-focused coping strategy that can reduce health risks and promote health resilience: Theory, review, and hypotheses. Psychology & Health, 19(3), 385–405.

Epilogue

The Victory Lap

Lessons from the Race

Key Learnings:

- Every stage of life, start, backstretch, curve, and home stretch, teaches a distinct form of wisdom.
- Success is not defined by pace but by purpose, resilience, and authenticity.
- Each stumble refines strength; each curve deepens character.
- Gratitude transforms experience into legacy.
- The race ends, but the lessons keep running through others.

Introduction: The Quiet After the Applause

The victory lap is unlike any other part of the race. The roar of the crowd fades, the stopwatch stops ticking, and yet something deeper begins. The runner walks now, not to prove anything, but to acknowledge what just happened. To honor the effort, the struggle, the pain, and the beauty of the run.

In life, the victory lap is the space between what was and what will always be the time of gratitude, reflection, and peace. It's when you realize that even though the race is over, its rhythm continues inside you.

Looking back, I see the full track now: the wild explosion of youth, the steady stride of adulthood, the curve of reinvention, the graceful slowing near the end. Every section demanded something different, but everyone mattered.

Lesson 1: The Start Teaches Courage

The start is about faith, the belief that the gun will sound and that you belong on the track. It's about shaking off hesitation, daring to begin even when you don't yet know how to finish.

Those early years taught that beginnings are never perfect. They're messy, uncertain, and full of mistakes, but movement is victory. The courage to begin remains one of life's most sacred acts.

In those days, courage was loud. Now, I know it can also be quiet; the steady kind that shows up again and again, regardless of applause.

Lesson 2: The Backstretch Teaches Endurance

The backstretch is where rhythm replaces excitement. It's where consistency matters more than intensity. Those middle years of responsibility spent building careers, raising families, and weathering storms were the longest part of the race.

Endurance meant learning to run while tired, to love while stretched, to serve even when unseen. It meant building strength not in sprints but in seasons.

And when the wind hit, I learned to lean not to fight life, but to move with it.

Lesson 3: The Curve Teaches Perspective

The curve changed everything. It taught me that speed without direction is wasted. The bend of life forced me to adjust form to release ego, embrace humility, and focus on meaning over motion.

It was on that curve that I found the wisdom of reinvention. I learned that the body slows, but the mind expands. That leadership is less about control and more about cultivation.

The curve taught that reflection is not retreat, it's refinement.

Lesson 4: The Home Stretch Teaches Peace

The home stretch is not about pushing it's about presence. It's where you realize that finishing well is better than finishing first.

Peace became the ultimate goal: peace with who I was, with who I became, and with what I will someday leave behind.

In that peace, gratitude bloomed. I stopped measuring days by what I accomplished and began measuring them by how deeply I lived.

The home stretch taught me to trade ambition for appreciation, and in doing so, I finally felt free.

Lesson 5: The Finish Teaches Light

The finish line revealed what had been true all along: the race was never about time; it was about transformation.

Crossing that invisible line, I imagine it not as darkness, but as light warm, vast, eternal. The same light that guided every step of the way. The same light that will carry my lessons forward through others.

In the end, the race didn't take something from me; it gave me everything.

Personal Reflections

When I began writing this, I thought of life as a race, a test of endurance, a battle against time. But now I see it as something else entirely.

It's choreography. It's movement through joy, pain, growth, and grace. Every stride taught rhythm, every rest taught reverence.

If I could speak to the younger version of myself standing on that starting line, I'd say: Run with curiosity. Don't fear the curve. When you stumble, rise with grace. When you reach the home stretch, slow down and smile. The race will end, but the light will continue.

Because somewhere, someone else is standing at their own starting line. And maybe, just maybe, something you left behind will help them run braver.

Conclusion: The Race That Never Ends

Life's race ends for each of us, but the lessons echo forever. We become part of the relay our stories, our examples, our kindness passed forward.

The victory lap isn't about being the fastest. It's about realizing that every lap was a privilege. It's the deep breath after the effort, the gratitude that fills the lungs where exhaustion once lived.

So take your victory lap. Smile. Wave to those who cheered you on and those who ran beside you. Let the applause fade into gratitude.

Because in the quiet after the finish, when the world slows and the track glows in the setting sun, you'll finally understand:

You didn't just run the race.

You became it.

References

Kübler-Ross, E. (1969). On death and dying. Macmillan.

McAdams, D. P. (2001). The psychology of life stories. Review of General Psychology, 5(2), 100–122.

Wong, P. T. P. (2010). Meaning therapy: An integrative and positive existential psychotherapy. Journal of Contemporary Psychotherapy, 40(2), 85–93.

Vaillant, G. E. (2002). Aging well: Surprising guideposts to a happier life from the Harvard study of adult development. Little, Brown and Company.

Frankl, V. E. (1959). Man's search for meaning. Beacon Press.

Acknowledgments

Writing Running the Curve has been more than a creative project. It has been a journey of gratitude, remembrance, and discovery.

To every athlete, student, colleague, and friend who ever stood with me on a track, in a classroom, or across a conversation, you helped shape the rhythm of this book. You reminded me that life's race is not a solo run, but a relay of influence, guidance, and shared humanity.

To my family, thank you for being the steady heartbeat behind every stride. For believing in the vision even when the pace slowed. For teaching me that love is the only finish line that matters.

To my mentors and peers in risk management, education, and leadership, your dedication to building safer, wiser spaces inspired the lessons that fill these pages. You helped me see that resilience is not a concept; it's a daily practice.

And to those whose names may never be printed here, but whose encouragement kept this work alive, thank you. You are part of this race, too.

Finally, to every reader who finds themselves somewhere between the start and the home stretch: may this book remind you that your curve, whatever it looks like, is worth running. Keep your form, trust your stride, and when in doubt, look toward the light.

Summary of Life's Four Quarters - A 400-Meter Metaphor for a Lifetime

Quarter	Age Range	Theme	Focus	Key Lessons
The Start (0–20)	Childhood & Adolescence	Acceleration	Foundation, curiosity, courage	Build habits, trust mentors, find your voice, begin with faith even when unsure.
The Backstretch (21–40)	Early & Mid-Adulthood	Endurance	Responsibility, rhythm, purpose	Learn to pace yourself, endure setbacks, balance ambition with rest, nurture relationships.
The Curve (41–60)	Maturity & Reinvention	Adaptation	Reflection, wisdom, reinvention	Adjust form, redefine success, prioritize health and meaning, embrace change as growth.
The Home Stretch (61–80+)	Legacy & Fulfillment	Grace	Peace, gratitude, teaching, closure	Slow with intention, savor life, forgive freely, pass the baton, finish with gratitude.

Reflection

The 400-meter race is demanding it requires speed, strategy, and soul. So does life. But just as in running, every section has its rhythm: the start builds faith, the backstretch builds strength, the curve builds wisdom, and the home stretch builds peace.

You don't have to run perfectly. You just have to keep running with heart, humility, and hope.

Because in the end, the true victory isn't in how fast you finished; it's in how deeply you lived.

Made in the USA
Las Vegas, NV
14 January 2026

38002325R00073